THE SECRET CODE
OF THE ODYSSEY

DID THE GREEKS SAIL THE ATLANTIC?

THE SECRET CODE

WITHDRAWN

OF THE ODYSSEY
GILBERT PILLOT

Translated from the French by FRANCIS E. ALBERT

Abelard-Schuman
London   New York   Toronto

Library of Congress Catalog Card Number: 77-141555
ISBN: 0 200 71773 1

Library of Congress Cataloging in Publication Data

Pillot, Gilbert.
  The secret code of the Odyssey.

  Translation of Le code secret de l'Odyssée.
  Bibliography: p.
  1. Homerus. Odyssea. I. Title.
PA4037.P5513   883'.01   77-141555
ISBN 0-200-71773-1

CONTENTS

LIST OF ILLUSTRATIONS

TRANSLATOR'S FOREWORD

If he is true to his trade, the translator of a book cannot help but become its most careful reader. While stripping the contents of its original linguistic symbols and clothing it in a new system of expressive signs, he acquires an intimacy with the author's thought that mere reading could hardly afford. Small wonder if his own impressions of a book change from the first casual reading until he has dwelt, as he must have, upon every paragraph, sentence and word.

"How delightful," I said, when the Senior Editor of Abelard-Schuman first approached me with the assignment. I truly relished the prospect of taking a few weeks' or months' vacation from our polluted twentieth century to sail with M. Pillot and Ulysses over unspoiled waters, on a fantastic adventure, the outcome of which seemed so beautifully irrelevant to the concerns of our world today. What difference, in fact, does it make to anybody, except archeologists, historians and literators, whether Ulysses sailed past Gibraltar, or, for that matter, whether he sailed at all?

As I now reach the end, I still think that M. Pillot's book with its direct and unpretentious style makes delightful reading, even though his technical accounts of navigational data might strain the mere layman's attention here and there, I still think that his answer to the riddle of the *Odyssey*, while provoking comment and controversy, will not change the course of modern history. But I was wrong in thinking that his analysis of a bygone world is irrelevant to ours. Reading *The Secret Code of the Odyssey* is bound to modify our personal understanding of Man, ancient and modern, and that may be a more exciting and useful achievement than the fragmented, petty, pragmatic chores most of us spend our lives performing.

Looking at Notre Dame in Paris, I have often wondered just how dark those Middle Ages really were when supposedly ignorant people, relying on nothing but their "spirit of faith," put stone upon stone until the pile, lo and behold, somehow became what it still is. I was even tempted once to ask a friend who is the contractor if he could design and build one of those cathedrals. Having now spent some time with Ulysses in myth-ridden antiquity when frightened people, we are taught to believe, expected the gods to look after them in every emergency, I am itching to ask my neighbor if he could drive his snowmobile from Pennsylvania to Las Vegas over snow-covered land, without benefit of compass and road map, *and* the Interstate highway system—relying on his gambling instinct for motivation, on the stars for guidance, and on his muscles for power, should his noisy engine break down as it undoubtedly would, long before he reached the Ohio border.

The Bronze-Age man who emerges from the Odyssey is an independent, crafty, knowledgeable, articulate, greedy, conniving, ambitious individual. He is capable of love and hatred, of soft words and thunder, of telling the truth and of lying. He is straightforward and corrupt, bloodthirsty and tender. He is ready to risk his life to save others or to kill others to save himself. He would punish by death a dozen indiscreet maidservants while he himself thinks nothing of sleeping with a golden-haired goddess he chances upon. He is so smart that he would have no trouble picking up New Math to help Telemachus with his homework, yet so utterly misguided that he would sacrifice comfort, home, peace, and scores of lives in the pursuit of a selfish dream of wealth and power. In other words, he is much like a lot of people you and I know, except that he is stronger and far more self-reliant, and that he gets a much larger share of living than most of us do.

If nothing else, *The Secret Code of the Odyssey* will help to put the fatuous myth of unqualified progress in the proper perspective. Granted that mankind has made some collective progress, at least in science and technology, the question is, how much progress have we made as individuals? How much of the collective knowledge do each of us effectively share? Most of all, how many of us would have the mental and physical equipment to cope with a not-so-motherly nature as these Ancients did? Along with "progress," the myth of the "generation gap" might also fall by the wayside. What kind of distance can twenty-five or thirty years measure, where there seems to be hardly any gap over several millenia? (One shudders at the thought that the Odyssey—this beguiling, corrupting, heroic, erotic, bloody poem—was required reading for countless generations of young Greeks, inciting their innocent minds to deeds of virtue and vice.)

If the foreword is mine, by courtesy of the publisher, the last word will undoubtedly be the reader's. He is entitled to know that this translation would be far more imperfect than it is, had it not been for the expert assistance of Dr. Rose Marie Marino of St. Louis University whose knowledge of the Mediterranean and of the languages involved helped me sail past many a potential Scylla and Charybdis.

F.E.A.

I. THE MESSAGE OF THE ODYSSEY

Yes, I am now finally convinced that the age of great adventure has not passed. It is possible to set out to discover not only islands and capes but also the sailors' terror, those whirlpools swirling in narrow straits amidst turbulent waters churned up, as legend has it, by some female demon hiding in a mysterious cave on the shore. Yes, it is possible to find the rocks of Scylla and Charybdis that Ulysses—according to Greek tradition recorded in Homer's *Odyssey*—sailed by twelve centuries before Christ.

I had been tempted for years to set out and identify, thirty centuries later, the places first discovered by Ulysses and his sailors. The idea was, no doubt, pretentious. Others before me had embarked on this venture and come to the firm conclusion that the countries of the Lotus-eaters, the Laestrygonians, and the Cimmerians, the island of Circe and far-away Ogygia, were situated along the coasts of Tunisia, Sicily, Sardinia, and Italy. The odds against my undertaking were extremely poor from the outset.

Around 1925, Victor Bernard combed through the *Odyssey* with scrupulous care and did a great deal (of field research to match up Homer and geography.) Had I been inspired at the beginning to read in detail his four-volume scholarly study, I would have probably abandoned my own project. I would have been intimidated by the mass of geographical and historical data that seemed to lend such weight to the author's claims. Fortunately, I had not seriously read the work until much later and so was free to steer an altogether different course.

My research first took the form of an intellectual adventure, the decoding of the *Odyssey*, followed by an actual survey of the seas in search of Charybdis and Scylla. Two events had a great deal to do with my decision to proceed.

An article in the twenty-second issue of *Planete* helped crystallize my intentions and theories. The author, historian Robert (Philippe,) claimed that the *Odyssey* could not possibly have had the Medittera-nean for its setting. There was no doubt, he said, that Ulysses sailed past Gibraltar and that the *Odyssey* was an account of a sea voyage to the north, mostly in the area of Brittany, I began myself to feel that previous theories confining Ulysses to the Mediterranean basin were wrong. I wished, therefore, to reread the *Odyssey* and try to confirm the Atlantic theory.

Other interests pushed my budding desire into the background until that birthday when my wife surprised me with a translation of the *Odyssey*. As I sat down that night to read Homer's poem, the very first lines brought my old problems back into focus. I was soon overwhelmed by the story, for the arrangement of the episodes, alternating precise geographical information with mythological ac-counts, suddenly made me feel that I was reading some sort of coded message I could not altogether decipher. From then on, the magic of the riddle, coupled with the joy of finding more and more answers, kept me breathless until I finally took off toward the misty north, following Ulysses' tracks. But let us not put the carriage before the horse. The first thing I did was to reread Homer—first the *Odyssey*, then the *Iliad*. What do these poems have to say to us today? What is their meaning?

Everyone knows the *Iliad* and the *Odyssey*. For many readers, these two poems, the oldest Greek texts available, stand simply for legend and mythology. The *Iliad* is a detailed account of the siege and fall of Troy. A succession of Achaean kings, or more exactly chieftains of the many principalities of ancient Greece, distinguish themselves in the long battle against the Trojans in which they fight with concerted effort in order to return flighty Helen, wife of King Menelaus of Lacedaemon, to her husband. After ten years of siege and fighting, King Ulysses of Ithaca conceives the idea of hiding with his soldiers inside a giant wooden horse that the Greek army, pretending retreat, abandons under the walls. Ulysses' gamble that the Trojans will then pull the horse inside the walls pays off; the Achaeans open the gates of the city to the awaiting troops that have in the meanwhile returned. The city is burned to the ground, and its people are massacred almost to the last inhabitant.

The Odyssey, chronologically, is a follow-up to the Iliad to which it is linked through Ulysses, its main character and the hero of the Trojan war, and in a more incidental manner through Telemachus's visit to various kings who come back to their homes after the war. Ulysses himself does not return with them. A storm drives him west and sets him on a long voyage fraught with danger and adventure. Twenty years go by before he finally returns to his native island where he and his son Telemachus kill the suitors, those pretenders who covet Penelope, his wife, and waste his fortune.

The Odyssey, on which my research was ultimately based, may be summed up as follows:

The story opens with Ulysses' return. He has just spent several years on a faraway island as a prisoner of the goddess Calypso.

He manages to build a ship, and lucky winds bring him back in seventeen days to the island of Scheria (Corfu) where Nausicaa, daughter of the Phaeacians' king, gives him shelter.

In the meantime, his son Telemachus is encouraged by Athene to sail from Ithaca to Pylos and inquire of Nestor about the fate of his father. From there he continues on to Sparta to ask the same of Menelaus.

On his return, he manages to avoid a trap set for him by the suitors of Ulysses' wife Penelope and finds the hut of a swineherd who remained loyal to Ulysses.

The Phaeacians treat Ulysses well. He agrees to tell his adventures if his hosts are willing to escort him to Ithaca the following day.

After the fall of Troy, Ulysses and his twelve ships sail around Cape Malea, the southernmost tip of the Peloponnesus. For nine days they sail off course, beyond Cythera. After visiting the land of the Lotus-eaters, they come upon an archipelago, some islands of which the Cyclôpes inhabit. Their leader, Polyphemus, a giant as big as a mountain, confines Ulysses and his crew in a cave, but they escape by clinging to the bellies of sheep after Ulysses blinds Polyphemus who has gotten drunk on Greek wine. In his rage, Polyphemus throws huge rocks at the ships as they sail away and calls down upon Ulysses the curse of Poseidon, master of the oceans and shaker of the earth.

The next stop is the island of Aea. Here Zephyr, the west wind, brings Ulysses within sight of Ithaca. His sailors are jealous of his luck and open the skins that contain the contrary winds. The ships are blown back to Aea.

A six-day trip then takes Ulysses to a famous port at the country of the Laestrygonians. Wild with rage, the Laestrygonians sink all of the ships that enter the harbor. The only one saved is Ulysses' craft, which stays outside the harbor, toward the open sea.

Ulysses and his sailors eventually land on the island of Aea, home of Circe the witch who detains them there a whole year.

As the days get longer again, Ulysses sets sail with the north wind (Boreas) and in one day reaches the country of the Cimmerians. He sails up the mouth of a river, anchors the ship, and conjures up the dead. He then returns to Circe in one night. The sorceress tells him the way to Greece. He should pass, but carefully avoid, the island of the Sirens, then follow a narrow strait through two islands where three times a day the waters come furiously alive with the whirlpool of Charybdis. It is vital to steer clear of Scylla, the horrible monster that lurks in a cave near the swirl. Ulysses follows the advice carefully and conquers the obstacles. He finally reaches the island of Thrinacia where Helios the sun god keeps his cattle at pasture. Headwinds stall the ship, and the hungry crew, ignoring Ulysses' warning, decide to slaughter the sacred cattle.

When they eventually put to sea again, Zeus, furious, strikes the ship by lightning. All of the sailors drown, Ulysses, hanging on to the wreckage of the ship, manages to stay alive.

Strong southerly winds drive him back in one night to the famous strait of Charybdis and Scylla.

He remains adrift with the wreckage for nine days and nights until he reaches the faraway island of Ogygia where the goddess Calypso gives him shelter.

The first scene of the homecoming, the visit to the Phaeacians, has already been described at the beginning of the *Odyssey*. The Phaeacians provide Ulysses with generous gifts and escort him back to Ithaca. He meets his son Telemachus at the swineherd's hut; with Athene's help, the two of them surprise the pretenders and slay them to the last.

The two poems, the *Iliad* and the *Odyssey*, are thus connected both through chronology and the main characters. The *Odyssey* makes frequent references to the Trojan War. When Ulysses calls up the spirits of the dead in the country of the Cimmerians, he is reunited for a moment with his former comrades of Troy who tell him how they have died. They evoke common memories.

Tradition ascribes these two epic poems to Homer. He is supposed to have created them in the eighth century B.C. from recitals sung by minstrels for several centuries. Since the events themselves are placed at the beginning of the twelfth century B.C., the memory of the heroic deeds of the Achaeans had been kept alive for four centuries by oral tradition before Homer set them down in writing. Such a time lag between events and their recording is a common phenomenon. *The Song of Roland*, for example, was composed in the twelfth century, but the event itself, the crossing of the Pyrenees at Roncesvalles, took place four centuries earlier, at the time of Charlemagne.

Some commentators question the existence of a "Homer." They claim that the two epics can be broken down into homogeneous segments easily identified by style and cast of characters. Thus the *Odyssey* is supposed to be a composite of three independent accounts: Ulysses' actual voyage; the voyage of Telemachus; and the events following Ulysses' homecoming to Ithaca. It really does not matter, though, whether "Homer" stands for one individual or a "staff" of poets commissioned to gather the current oral accounts and check their reliability. Their work did yield a coherent text that incorporates the songs they found to be the most genuine. The main thing is that, judging by the results, the work was done with the greatest care. Two reasons seem to rule out any doubt about this.

First of all, one must keep in mind that the stakes of a writers' effort were very high. The Greek cities that claim Homer for their native son are in Asia Minor. At Homer's time, they had been populated for several centuries by Greek immigrants who settled the area following the Dorian invasion at the beginning of the Iron Age. The songs of the *Iliad* and the *Odyssey* are part of their cultural heritage, they remind them of the history of their people and the great deeds of their ancestors. These cities, rivals in business and jealous of their political independence, were able to find their common national identity as Greeks precisely through the knowledge of a glorious past shared by all. Very likely, the poet was deeply conscious of the cultural and historical relevance of his work and considered his mission sacred.

For another reason, the narrative as a whole is so smooth and coherent that there can be little doubt of its basic unity despite some differences in style. Before the story begins to unfold, the goddess Athene sums up the events to be told, outlines the setting, and names the cast. In a matter of days, then, two simultaneous events are brought about by the will of the gods; Telemachus's voyage and the return of Ulysses with the elaborate account of his adventures. Finally the two protagonists, father and son, team up for the last act, the slaughter of the suitors. The particular events that make up each of the three phases follow an almost minute-by-minute schedule. The very frequent insistence throughout the text on details of time and place reinforce the impression that the events follow a mechanical, rigorous plan designed to synchronize the activities of father and son. We shall see later what conclusions can be drawn from this parallelism, and especially from the conscious effort to relate the return of Ulysses to the voyage of Telemachus. Incidentally, Telemachus's trip yields no particular results, adds nothing to the action, and is irrelevant to the sequence of events. At the same time, it abounds in precise geographical details and measurements of time and distances covered. It will thus be quite natural for me to adopt the theory that this incidental account has no other purpose than to supply the clues for understanding the main story, the voyage of Ulysses.

The reader may wonder why we need clues in the first place in order to understand the *Odyssey*. It goes without saying that as long as we consider the *Odyssey* a mythological legend, a work of fiction in poetic form, there is no need for keys, nor for any research for that matter. If that is the case, either concern over the likelihood of the story or the attempt to localize the events would be quite futile. In that hypothesis, readers and commentators could not do much more than examine the feelings experienced, the psychological behavior of the characters, and the external form of the account as a poem. On the other hand, many authors today agree that legends, transmitted orally for centuries, then recoded and recopied, invariably yield, despite the inevitable material errors, a core of historical truth since their basic intent is to record the most important events of the life of a people. The Bible, which predated Homer's work, tells the story of the various Jewish tribes, and many topographical data connected with the events have been verified by archeological discoveries. As long as topographical descriptions can be verified on the spot, there is no reason to deny that which is not subject to direct verification, that is, events to which these very places testify.

Research to verify the *Iliad* has been carried out. The German archeologist Schliemann, starting out with nothing but Homer's text, was able to find the city of Troy under the hill of Hissarlik in Asia Minor, not far from the Dardanelles. Since this discovery, no one would doubt that Homer's Iliad is a true story. The Trojan War, the siege and destruction of the city, suddenly ceased to be a legend and became history. It would be strange, then, to suppose that the *Odyssey*, which is a follow-up to the *Iliad* and has always been associated with it, is nothing but legend mixed with mythology. It is far more likely that the second story is also an account of historical events that took place during the twelfth century B.C., a few years after the fall of Troy, which historians place at about 1180 B.C. Finally, one might add, in support of the theory, that generations of Greeks have for centuries handed down these stories, collected them, put them in writing, and learned them by heart as children. Would people have handled with such care legends that everybody knew were pure fiction? With the information we have today about the way people lived and thought during the high Greek Middle Ages, it is hard to believe that the mere poetic charm of the songs of the

Odyssey could account for all the care in their transcription and in the preservation of the epic.

For all of those who took the trouble of memorizing it at an age when few knew how to read and write, the meaning of the message and the recital of the events themselves must have been far more important than the form.

Once we admit that the Iliad speaks of historical events, there is no problem in interpreting and understanding the epic. The same is not true of the *Odyssey*, the very core of which, Ulysses' voyage, has remained to this day a real puzzle. An explanation becomes possible, however, if we suppose that the *Odyssey* contains a message meant only for the initiated. The obvious theory relates to a sea expedition that actually took place, a western replica of the Trojan expedition to the east on which the Greeks embarked in order to conquer the Bosporus and the Black Sea. The success of this first undertaking would have inspired them to set out to the west on another adventure in order to gain control of some traditional trade routes well known especially to their Cretan predecessors. However important the story of an expedition, or a geographical discovery at the moment it is made, it may still be the account of a purely incidental event without future and with little relevance to the history of a people.

The message of the *Odyssey* could have been a more important one for the contemporaries and especially for their descendants. This could well have been the case if Ulysses' voyage were not simply a tale of a chanceful adventure, but rather a pretext to describe a sea route on which the prosperity and power of a nation may have depended. At the time of seafaring by sail, mariners could not reach their destination unless they knew winds and currents well, and sea routes were jealously guarded secrets. Sailors of the same nationality, however, must have exchanged by oral tradition information concerning the routes to follow. One simple way of preventing "leaks" was to conceal the reports within a much larger story and disperse in other songs additional information without which the itinerary would not be understood. Thus, only those who knew by heart the entire text were able to select and gather the necessary data, carry out other pertinent calculations, and determine with precision the route to follow.

The *Odyssey*, then, is both the narrative of an ill-fated expedition and the description of a maritime route. Convinced as I am, I will attempt to lift the veil that shrouds Ulysses' voyage, hunt for the key to the message, and try to decipher the actual secret of this astonishing adventure: the Atlantic route heading for the northwest of Europe.

II. THE KEYS TO THE ODYSSEY

Let us sum up the basic elements of the problem. The subject matter is a fabulous sea voyage. We learn about it by listening to Ulysses as he tells the story to the Phaeacians. These people live on the island of Scheria and are themselves great seamen, "lovers of oars" and "ferrymen," as Homer reminds us on several occasions.

The story is a puzzling one. It is enough to read the account just once to conclude that, in effect, Ulysses talks two different languages, switching back and forth between them throughout the narrative. One is the language of mythology in which he tells us about some rather incredible happenings that seem to belong in the realm of fancy and poetry. The other language is a practical and concrete one and supplies topographical information about land and sea with astonishing detail and accuracy. I would like to emphasize from the outset that Ulysses keeps using this double language in describing each episode of the trip. This would lead one to think that each is supposed to convey partial information that a knowledgeable audience can put together in order to decipher the true meaning of the message. When I started my research on the *Odyssey*, I had few tools at my disposal for a meaningful interpretation of mythological events. I decided, therefore, to concentrate first on those precise data the interpretation of which was obvious and certain. These fall essentially into two categories: reports on places visited and nautical data of course and time.

It is abundantly clear, first of all, that we are dealing with a long voyage that covers great distances. On most legs of the journey, Ulysses travels day and night. Thus, for example, on the return trip

An ancient bas-relief showing Ulysses bound to the mast of his ship.   *Photo:*
Giraudon

from the island of Ogygia where he has spent seven years as Calypso's
guest, he travels seventeen days before reaching the island of Scheria.
Now, the ancients themselves thought, with good reason, that Scheria
was nothing else than Corfu. But where was Ulysses coming *from*?

Let us figure on a speed of five to six knots an hour. At this
relatively modest speed, a sailing ship will cover some 150 nautical
miles in 24 hours, or close to 4,600 kilometers in 17 days, which
would take us a good distance beyond Gibraltar. Taking into account
some additional data, such as fog, ground swell, and the tide, which
rises three times a day at Charybdis, historian Robert (Philippe) came
to the conclusion in an article published in *Planete* that Ulysses must
have sailed out to the Atlantic Ocean and that all previous commen-
taries were warped by the gratuitous confining of the trip to the
Mediterranean.

Commentators have traditionally sought to chart Ulysses' trip around Sicily and the southern tip of the Italian peninsula. Now, the various theories on distances and course do not dovetail with Homer's text. In addition, recent archeological findings have established that all of these places, since they are at a few days' distance from Greece, had long been familiar to the Cretes and the Mycenaeans. The *Odyssey* mentions a plan to send Ulysses to visit the Sicilians; the obvious implication one draws is that a trip around the well-known island could not conceivably have developed into such a fantastic adventure.

Authors have insisted that the famous passage of Charybdis and Scylla is nothing else than the Strait of Messina between Sicily and Calabria. They seem to forget that the text does not speak of a strait but of two islands, that Ulysses' description bears no resemblance to the actual topography of these sites.

We thus have no choice concerning Ulysses' voyage but to get away from this Mediterranean theory that for two thousand years has kept Homer's commentators locked in a maze of contradictions. We must be daring enough to tackle the problem from a wider angle, adopting a strict method.

I take Robert (Philippe's) Atlantic theory for my general guide. I submit that on this basis we ought to select and admit in evidence only those precise data of time and course that allow us to sketch Ulysses' itinerary first in a general way.

The second task will be to discover the "scale" of this sketch and determine the exact distances covered in the various directions. Only then shall I proceed to study a modern map and personally visit the areas described in order to find the exact places where Ulysses has stopped, especially the rocks of Scylla and Charybdis of which he gives a very precise description. If I can thus establish the route followed by Ulysses, I should be able to understand the meaning of the trip, to interpret it correctly and look for its ultimate "motive." And if it turns out that Homer's poetic text actually hides a historical message meant for the posterity of the Achaeans, we will have achieved a better understanding of ancient Greece, of the thoughts of her people and the level of their knowledge. We will be able to explain more clearly the "Greek miracle" of the fifth century B.C., this sudden booming of intellectual activity and the flowering of scientific consciousness that constitute the foundations of our own civilization.

If we are to chart Ulysses' seaway, we must determine two essential factors for each leg of the trip: course followed and distance covered.

Homer has two ways of recording a nautical course. Most often he indicates the direction from which the wind blows. We know today that in Homer's time ships could only sail ahead of the wind. The techniques of sailing into the wind had not been discovered until much later, with the advent of the Latin sail. The square sail with which Ulysses' ships were equipped could take advantage only of favorable winds, which for them meant winds propelling them from the rear. Otherwise, they had to rely on oars.

When Homer says that the ships were chased by a strong "Boreas," the Greek name for the north wind, I take this to mean that the ships were headed south. There is a convincing proof of this at the beginning of Ulysses' story. As he leaves the Ciconians' country, situated to the north of the Aegean sea, he is heading toward Cape Malea, riding with Boreas. In the same manner, when Zephyr, Eurus, or Notus blow, that is, the west, east, or south winds, I take it the ships are headed east, west, or north. So, interpreting the text in these cases is a relatively simple task.

Homer uses another method as well. When Ulysses, on his way home, leaves the island of Ogygia, the refuge of Calypso, the goddess advises him to keep the Big Dipper constantly on his left. If we check the positions of the stars three thousand years ago on a fall night, which was the time Ulysses set sail, we can conclude that the Big Dipper, which describes an apparent circle around the polar star every 24 hours, was then in the eastern half of the sky. If Ulysses could see the Big Dipper on his left at night, he must have been facing south and following a north-south course as he leaves the island of Calypso. Homer notes also that Ulysses was "looking at the Pleiades." It so happens that at midnight at that time of the year this constellation is exactly to the south. The very location of the island confirms the theory of a north-south course. Two important remarks in the text lead us to conclude that the island is situated at a high latitude. First we have the account of Zeus's sending Hermes as a messenger to persuade Calypso to let Ulysses return home to Ithaca. Hermes takes off from Mt. Olympus and flies over Pieria. It occurred to me to draw a line from Mt. Olympus to the highest peak of the Pieria range. What I got was a direct northwest bearing. On a map of Greece, the line cuts across the meridians at a precise 45-degree angle.

The other indication concerns the latitude at which the island is situated. We have pointed out that the Big Dipper is the only constellation that remains visible as it describes a circle around the polar star with the rotation of the earth. A person standing at the North Pole would have the polar star directly overhead, with all the stars turning around it in a circle and none sinking below the horizon. Watching it from a point on the equator, the polar star is at the horizon, and the other stars describe a semicircle around it, rising in the east and setting in the west. At latitudes between the pole and the equator, the polar star appears somewhere between the vertical and the horizontal. The vertical degree between the horizon and the polar star indicates the latitude of the place from which the measurement is taken. The stars closest to the polar star trace a full circle, while constellations situated farther away from the center sink every night into the ocean.

Homer also says that "Aries sets late," meaning that the constellation Aries barely touches the ocean and stays only a short time under the horizon as it follows its daily movement around the polar star. Now, the part of the earth where these conditions are met must be somewhere between northern latitudes 60 and 65. As it happens, Iceland would fit all three conditions perfectly. It is an island; it is located between the 60th and 65th parallels; it lies exactly to the northwest of Mt. Olympus. All of this might be just a troublesome coincidence. If it is not, Iceland's entering the picture is such an unexpected development because of the island's distance from Greece that I cannot consider it seriously without further proof.

There are two data, however, that I found completely reliable. Ogygia, Calypso's island, is definitely situated along a high northern parallel. And when Ulysses leaves the island, he is definitely headed south.

I am going to draw a four-column chart and one by one enter for each lap of the trip the course followed by the ships when this is indicated by the winds or by some other reference, and also the elapsed time that Homer usually expresses in terms of days of navigation. I thus jot down a line for the homeward trip of Ulysses that we hear about in the beginning of the story:

From the Island of Calypso to the Island of Scheria:
North-South Course at the Start—17 days

I will then examine one by one the incidents of the trip that Ulysses elaborates on from the ninth book. I will note on my chart all the certain information concerning course and time, forgetting about the mythological adventures that at first appeared to me irrelevant to the actual itinerary.

Let me begin with the first leg of the trip. The route is quite clear from Troy to the Ciconians' country and to Cape Malea. The reference to the wind of Boreas confirms the north-south course, as does a check of the map of Greece. Ulysses' fleet wastes no time crossing the Aegean Sea from Thrace to the Peloponnesus and it is about to sail around Cape Malea, the southern tip of the Peloponnesus, on an east-west course in order then to turn northwest toward Ithaca. Sailors of the time knew very well the great hazards of rounding the cape. At this point in Ulysses' trip, a storm rises and pushes the ships beyond the island of Cythera, that is, in a westerly direction. For nine days, they run with the wind and eventually put in at the Lotus-eaters' country, which Ulysses calls a continent and not an island as some have thought. This lap is entered on the chart in the following words:

Cythera to the Lotus-eaters: East-West
Probable—9 Days (a Continent)

On the tenth day, Ulysses and his companions spend part of the day among the Lotus-eaters, then suddenly put to sea again and reach by nightfall one of the islands of the archipelago where the Cyclôpes live. They pick the one island that is deserted.

Here I cannot enter a course since none is indicated in the *Odyssey*, I am merely going to note the estimated elapsed time, that is, 6 hours or one quarter of a 24-hour day.

From the Lotus-eaters to the Islands of the Cyclôpes: 1/4 day

The sailors get into a fight with Polyphemus; the giant throws huge stones at the fleet as it tries to put to sea. The ships eventually reach the island of Aeolia by rowing. The island must be rather close since Ulysses makes no reference to days of sailing. Other than that there are no precise data for this lap.

Upon leaving the island of Aeolia, Ulysses is at the helm day and night and is being chased by Zephyr (west wind) for nine days without a stop. At daybreak of the tenth day, he sights the coast of Ithaca. His sailors untie the skins that hold the opposite winds and the ships are immediately blown back toward Aeolia.

This strange episode appeared to me at the very first reading as both important and exceptional one—important because it marks the first time that Ulysses supplies precise coordinates by reference to a known territory. It is clear, in fact, that the island of Aeolia is 9 days' sailing time to the west of Ithaca, a sailing day meaning day and night, or 24 hours. Yet the episode is a strange one indeed, and the quick round trip seems to complicate the voyage uselessly at a point where Ulysses had already gone so far away from home. It appears an improbable feat, also, from the viewpoint of navigation. All through the narrative, the mythological episodes appear to me evidently incredible, as they must have appeared to the Greeks at the time, unless I altogether miss their real meaning. But up to this point the topographical and nautical references have always been very precise whether they dealt with maneuvers of putting to sea or to port, or with some deep-water shelter securely hidden along a coast. When I compare this account to the rest of the story, I hear a false ring that is out of tune with both geography and navigation. What could have been its actual intent? We ought to keep in mind that the epic is meant for an audience of sailors who knew their business and could "tell good grain from bad," true from false. On these premises,

I think it likely that the episode is inserted because it carries important information, the location of the island of Aeolia, that is undoubtedly one of the main keys to the whole trip. It is, in fact, the only place along the route where we can refer to a known point, Ithaca. So I make another entry on the chart:

Island of Aeolia to Ithaca: West-East 9 Days
Ithaca to Island of Aeolia: East-West 9 Days

If this is so, things begin to make more sense. The poet makes sure to convey to us a valuable reference of course and time. He would not have done so if somewhere in the narrative there were not some clues allowing the conversion of days of sailing into distance, or the information would have been completely meaningless. At this point in my reasoning I could follow either one of two paths. Yielding to impatience, I could attempt to discover and geographically locate a solid point on the itinerary, then set out immediately to find the key, which, as I suspected, should not be too difficult to discover. Or I had the choice of following the path of method and wisdom, continuing with my chart to the end without letting myself be drawn away from my appointed task. I take advantage, though, of the Aeolia episode to point out that Ulysses' route definitely points to the west. The westerly direction from Cape Malea to the Lotuseaters, which I marked as merely probable on my chart, now seems to be confirmed.

I am more and more convinced that a ship setting sail from Greece and running westward ahead of a storm for nine days and nights would cover a distance that takes her without a doubt beyond Hercules' Columns, or Gibraltar in the Achaeans' language. It doesn't take too long to figure out that a ship sailing at the speed of 8 knots per hour, which is not excessive for a ship pushed by gale-force winds, would cover a distance of about 200 miles in 24 hours or more than 3,000 kilometers in 9 days. Now the Strait of Gibraltar is about 2,500 kilometers west of Cape Malea. We must discard the idea that the whole voyage took place within the Mediterranean Sea. But after this parenthesis I must get back to the itinerary and finish my chart of course and sailing time.

After leaving the island of Aeolia, Ulysses and his companions sail for six days. On the seventh day, they put in at Laestrygonian country in a famous harbor located within a bay almost completely closed to the open sea by overhanging cliffs.

In this country, "herdsman hails herdsman as one brings in his droves and the other answers as he drives out his, and a man who could do without sleep, could earn double wages." This remark clearly indicates that Ulysses is impressed by the length of daylight, which, counting a working day of eight hours, must have lasted at least sixteen hours. The event must have taken place at the beginning of the summer since the Greeks did not sail during the bad season. We must suppose that this country is located far up to the north, and that Ulysses' fleet, upon leaving the island of Aeolia, followed a northerly course, give or take a few degrees in that general direction. For this lap, I am going to enter on my chart:

Island of Aeolia to Laestrygonians:
Approximate Northerly Course: 6 Days

After a stunning defeat that cost him all of his ships except one, Ulysses "sails on" until he reaches the island of Aea where the goddess Circe lives. The expression "sails on" might mean that Ulysses follows the same bearing as on a previous leg, although this next one must be rather short since there is no reference to its length in the usual terms of days of sailing. It would seem, therefore, that he continues on northward. My entry for this leg:

Laestrygonians to the Island of Circe
Approximate South-North Course: Duration Unknown

The island of Circe is strewn with valleys and is rather small and practically circular, for Ulysses, from a vantage point on the top of the highest hill, notes that the sea surrounds the island like a brilliant belt. Under normal conditions of visibility at that latitude, the island does not appear to be more than six to eight miles across at its widest point. Ulysses' description makes it also clear that there are no high mountains on the island.

He spends the winter on the island and, following Circe's advice to visit the Cimmerians' country, sets sail again. He leaves in the morning and travels through the day, with Boreas helping him. The bearing is clear: The Cimmerian country is a half-day trip from the island of Circe. Thus the entry is:

Island of Circe to Cimmerians:
North-South: One Half Day

I would like to point out incidentally to what extent the techniques of sailing are respected. Coming as he is from the island of Circe, that is, from the high sea, since the island is a small one, Ulysses takes advantage of the daytime when the wind blows toward the coast. On the next day, he sets out in the evening to sail back to the island of Circe. Another entry on the chart:

Cimmerians to Island of Circe:
South-North Course: One Half Day

When Ulysses was heading toward the island of Circe the first time, he could not have been following a due-north bearing. The Cimmerians' country is south of the island of Circe, and Ulysses would have sighted that coast at the first passage. He must have been traveling, therefore, at a slight angle east or west of a generally north course.

As he leaves Circe again, he puts to sea at dawn and sails past the island of the Sirens. He also passes by Charybdis and Scylla, and at nightfall arrives at the islant of Trident where he is stranded for a while due to bad weather. Since I have no data here on course, I can only note on the chart the one certain piece of information: This leg of the trip lasted from dawn to dusk, or took one half of a 24-hour day.

Island of Circe to the Island of Trident: One Half Day

Ulysses leaves Trident, and his ship is destroyed by lightning. Notus drives him and the wreckage back to Charybdis and Scylla in one night. This detail allows me to conclude that Ulysses had been heading south, passing first along the whirlpool of Charybdis and then the cave of Scylla, and that the island of Trident is a few hours' distance to the south, southeast, or southwest of the notorious passage. Which yields the following on the chart:

Island of Trident to Charybdis and Scylla:

South-North—a Few Hours of Sailing or Half a Day of Drifting

As I put this down on paper, I become aware of a new problem: the day Ulysses spent adrift on the sea. Up to now, distances were always expressed in terms of sailing days. This convenient unit of measure was the key to the message and the only problem was to find its equivalent in distance. The drift complicates the problem. I checked and rechecked Homer's report on the round trip between the cave of Scylla and the island of Trident, looking for a clue to draw a parallel between the two units of measurement. The two trips seem practically the same, although we have no certain information on the location of the shipwreck. The trip down could not have taken more than a few hours since Ulysses mentions that after escaping from the whirlpool of Charybdis he very soon reaches the island of Trident. On the other hand, he is drifting all through the night with the wreck before he is back to the same spot. The information is so vague that no precise parallel can be established. I have no choice but to enter this new unit on the chart and hope that Homer will soon throw some light on the problem, which he eventually will. In the meantime, I must be satisfied with stating the new measure, hoping that a clue will soon turn up.

Ulysses passes once again between Charybdis and Scylla and remains adrift for nine days and nights before he is washed ashore at the island of Ogygia where Calypso receives him. I have the following to add to my chart:

Charybdis and Scylla to the Island of Calypso:
9 Days of Drifting

As I reread this entry, I notice that I can draw some conclusions concerning the position of the island of Circe in reference to Charybdis and Scylla.

It seems clear from the outset that this island must be situated north of the two dangerous reefs. When Ulysses leaves them behind the first time, he is headed south, so at any rate a southerly position must be ruled out. Neither can the island be exactly to the north, for Ulysses would have passed through the reefs on his north-south trip to the Cimmerians' country, which he did not since he says nothing about it at that time.

The island of Circe must then be to the northwest or northeast of Charybdis and Scylla, which themselves are to the northwest or northeast of the island of Trident.

Finally, that Ulysses drifts by the reefs with a south wind makes us suspect that the 9-day drifting was liable to take him to even higher latitudes than he had reached before.

A valuable piece of information helps up specify the latitude of Scylla and Charybdis. Charybdis is evidently a whirlpool caused by tidal currents among reefs scattered along a rocky shoreline. Now, Ulysses tells us that this phenomenon occurs "three times a day." We know that after spending the winter with Circe he sets sail "when the seasons come round again," which could be interpreted at a time about the June solstice. With high and low tides alternating every six hours, the day must have lasted about eighteen hours. The corresponding northern latitude could evidently vary several degrees, depending on what is meant by "day." We have thus an area anywhere between 55 and 60 degrees of northern latitude, the precise location depending on whether "day" means light and includes dawn and dusk or indicates the time elapsed between the actual rising and setting of the sun.

I am personally inclined toward the second interpretation and would prefer to place Charybdis and Scylla with the neighboring islands of Circe and Trident between 55 and 58 degrees of northern latitude.

I have already spoken of course and time involved in Ulysses' long homeward voyage from the island of Ogygia to the island of Scheria, which is no doubt the same as Corfu. I quote here as a reminder a previous entry on the chart:

From the Island of Calypso to the Island of Corfu:
North-South Course at the Start: 17 Days

If I keep in mind that Ulysses had sailed westward for 9 days before turning north, I find it evident that on the homeward trip from a probably high latitude he must follow rather closely the same itinerary, that is, sail first toward the south until he reaches the latitude of Greece and then turn eastward.

As the next step, I took my finished chart with all the essential information on directions and time of sailing and I started a little

game, trying to outline all the possible itineraries that would meet
the conditions described above. To determine the distances covered, I
take a day of sailing as a unit and assign to it a certain length. These
outlines could only give a general idea of directions followed and
serve merely to clarify ideas and eliminate contradictions. They could
serve as a tool to establish the exact proportions of the itinerary for
various reasons, two of which are decisive. First, even if we should
adopt an indefinite day of navigation for a scale, we still would not
know the precise distances covered because of the curvature of the
earth, which cannot be represented on a two-dimensional plan. Then,
we still lack certain necessary data, and any reference to distances
covered can only be a theory when the number of sailing days is not
specified.

After drawing several sketches, I turn again to Homer's story in
search of clues that are likely to supply the true scale of the
itinerary, that is the distance covered in 24 hours of sailing and in 9
days of drifting on the sea.

This step in my research has definitely yielded one first concrete
result. All the tentative sketches that I drew on the basis of the
information recorded on the chart took the general shape of a capital
L. Adding to this the topographical indications I was able to find, I
had no choice but to discard once and for all the theory confining
the voyage to the Mediterranean Sea. I had already come to the
tentative conclusion that we must leave the Mediterranean basin when
I first realized how great a distance Ulysses must have covered on his
homebound trip from the island of Ogygia, running as he was for
seventeen days ahead of the wind.

There is also the puzzling reference to the length of the day in
the Laestrygonians' country where "a man who could do without
sleep could earn double wages." It would be difficult to find a place
anywhere in the Mediterranean where a June day would be that long.

Then there is the fact that the sign of Aries barely touches the
ocean, which indicates a latitude north of 60°. The phenomenon of
Charybdis further points to the fact that we are in a sea where the
tide brings about violent coastal currents.

I had the feeling, however, that all of these arguments in favor of
an Atlantic theory would remain mere assumptions unless I could

specify the exact scale of the general sketch. After that I could look for additional support by studying the maps and attempting to reconcile the itinerary as calculated with the actual geographical data.

The most important task was to discover a first clue that I needed for establishing a scale, that is, for specifying the distance covered by a ship in one day and one night, or in twenty-four hours of navigation ahead of the wind. Now, in Ulysses' voyage we do not know the distances and are therefore unable to pinpoint the speed of the ships. I wondered then if we could not find some clue in the account of Telemachus's voyage to sandy Pylos, which took place during Ulysses' homebound trip. Here Homer speaks of places within Greece itself that are well known to the audience. If sailing times are recorded with sufficient precision, the audience should be able to measure the distances covered, determine the speed of the ships, and transpose these data to the main story.

I will attempt to calculate the time elapsed in the trip and the distance covered for Telemachus's round trip between Ithaca and Pylos.

Telemachus leaves Ithaca in the evening and reaches Pylos at sunrise. He covers about 130 kilometers, or in Greek measure 700 stades exactly, one stade equaling about 185 meters. Knowing that 600 stades equal one geographical degree of latitude (since longitudinal degrees vary according to latitude) the distance covered by Telemachus equals exactly one and one-sixth of a degree.

On the return trip, Telemachus puts to sea at Pylos after spending the night inland and steers to the north following the west coast of the Peloponnesus. At sunset he is near the western cape of (Elia) from which he navigates toward the Pointed islands. These are located to the north of that area at the other side of the entrance to the Gulf of Corinth. The purpose of this maneuver was to avoid a direct course that would have led him into the trap set by the pretenders who lied in wait for him near the small island of Asteris to the south of Ithaca.

The distance covered from Pylos until sunset amounts to 65 kilometers, or 350 stades, which disposes of the problem of distance. Now I have to determine the time elapsed.

In both cases I know the exact hours of arrival, indicated in terms of sunrise and sunset. Since the events take place at the beginning of fall, we can assume that the day and the night each last twelve hours. If I can also determine the exact time of departure in each case, I will know how long the trip actually took. Until now the problem appeared relatively simple, but as we are going to see, the task of determining the hours of departure will involve us in somewhat more complex calculations.

Let us recall that at the time of departure from Ithaca, "the sun went down and the streets were all darkened" when Athene made her way to the house of Ulysses and called Telemachus to follow her down to the port. There a ship and a crew are waiting. The sailors and Telemachus return to the house to fetch the provisions for the trip. When all is put on board, they lose no time casting off.

From sunset Athene walks the distance between the harbor and the house of Ulysses four times. The ancient Greeks may have understood the distances involved. To me this was just another unknown quantity; the only thing I could do was to search the text further for an answer. Reference is made several times to people leaving the city to go to Ulysses' house and vice versa, which leads us to believe that the house was somewhere outside the city. When Eumaeus the swineherd, sent by Ulysses and Telemachus, arrives to announce Telemachus's return, one of the pretenders is next to Penelope and sees from the porch of the house the ship of the pretenders as it enters the harbor. The indication that I sought will become clear with a careful analysis of this passage. To understand the episode we must follow the events on a detailed map of Ithaca and establish an accurate chronological sequence. At sunrise Ulysses and Telemachus are with Eumaeus the swineherd at the southern end of the island across form the city of (Samos) on the other side of the strait separating Ithaca from Cephalonia. Telemachus's ship leaves the shore to reach the port of Ithaca by rounding the southern tip of the island while Eumaeus the swineherd starts out on foot across the island toward the house of Ulysses. At the same time, the pretenders are waiting in ambush about 6 kilometers to the south of the same point on the other side of the strait. The swineherd, the ship of

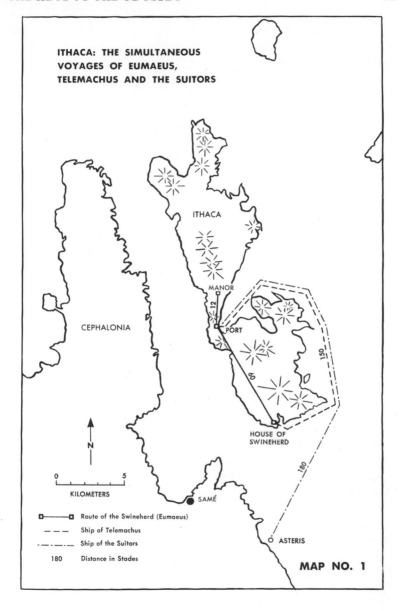

ITHACA: THE SIMULTANEOUS
VOYAGES OF EUMAEUS,
TELEMACHUS AND THE SUITORS

ITHACA

MANOR

12

CEPHALONIA

PORT

150

80

HOUSE OF
SWINEHERD

180

N

0   5

KILOMETERS

SAMÉ

◻━━━◻   Route of the Swineherd (Eumaeus)
━ ━ ━   Ship of Telemachus
━·━·━   Ship of the Suitors
180   Distance in Stades

○ ASTERIS

MAP NO. 1

Telemachus, and the pretenders *start out at the same exact time*. Eumaeus takes off on foot by the mountain roads to reach the house of Ulysses, which must be to the northwest of the city since upon his return he says that he had gone through the city in order to reach the house. He is therefore going first to the city and then to the house.

When the pretenders see Telemachus's ship, most probably as it is rounding the tip, they leave their hideout and set out back to Ithaca where they arrive shortly after Telemachus. Eumaeus and another messenger from Telemachus's ship reach Penelope at the same time and bring her the news. Penelope warns the other group of pretenders who are at the house that her son has returned. The pretenders discuss the matter and decide that they should notify the ones waiting in ambush on board ship that there is no need to wait any longer. One of them gets up, walks out the door, and tells the rest of the group that such a warning would be useless because the ship is in port and they can see their friends taking in the sails and pulling up the oars.

When the swineherd arrives back to Ulysses "at nightfall," he reports that from the top of the hill of Hermes, overlooking the harbor area, he saw the pretenders' ship as it was entering the harbor. This incident precedes by a short time the one I had just described since the ship is just entering the port. Therefore, the hill of Hermes must be close to the house of Ulysses.

Thus the pretenders' ship must be entering the port about the time when Eumaeus and the other messenger reach the house and Penelope. This yields a first conclusion that is interesting to note: *The time the messenger took to climb from the port to the house equals the time of delay of the pretenders' ship behind Telemachus.* Another important point of information: The swineherd starts out on his walk early in the morning and is back to his original point of departure by "nightfall." *He has been walking all through the day*. Homer is careful to point out that Eumaeus did not stop on the way, for the swineherd had suggested he make a detour in order to notify Laertes, the father of Ulysses, but Telemachus insisted that he come directly back.

I shall now try to determine the distance covered. According to the map, the distance between the south of the island and the port that is situated along the east coast at the middle of Ithaca is about 11 kilometers, or 60 stades. At the same time, the ship of Telemachus, which sails around and must avoid shoals and capes, must cover about 28 kilometers or 150 stades. We know that the time Eumaeus and the messenger take to reach the house of Penelope from the port is the same as the time of delay of the pretenders' arrival after Telemachus. Now, the pretenders must cover a longer course, perhaps 5 to 6 kilometers longer, which would bring their trip to 180 stades or one-fifth longer than Telemachus's.

If the swineherd walks at a steady pace, the distance covered by him and the messenger from the harbor to the house of Ulysses equals one-fifth of the distance Eumaeus has already covered, or 12 stades. The distance covered by Eumaeus by land equals, therefore, 60 + 12 = 72 stades to go, and the same to return, or 144 stades in 12 hours. He is walking at an average speed of 12 stades per hour and takes one hour to reach the house of Ulysses from the port. This speed equals 2.25 kilometers per hour, which seems to be normal for a man walking on mountain paths, especially for an elderly shepherd who must take it easy in order to be able to walk all day long without stopping. What this calculation yields is that Eumaeus the swineherd, leaving at 6 A.M., arrived at his destination at noon, having climbed for one hour from the port to the house between 11 A.M. and noon.

Applying this figure to Telemachus's trip, I can conclude that two round trips between the ship and the house of Ulysses must have taken two hours. In other words, Telemachus left Ithaca four hours after sunset. Since his ship reaches sandy Pylos at sunrise, it has traveled for eight hours to cover a distance of 700 stades, or one and one-sixth of a geographical degree. In 24 hours, he could have covered three times that distance, *2,100 stades or three and one-half geographical degrees*.

Having thus established this first result, I am obviously tempted to find out how fast the ships were traveling. One may wonder at this point whether my decision will be a likely one, or even relevant.

It is possible after all that my figuring is based on merely chanceful data. Homer could be describing the various sunrises and sunsets for no other reason than to enhance his images and make the story more colorful. Yet it is interesting to note that these phenomena always occur at the precise times that also mark the various legs of the trips and at points that are easily identified on the map.

This observation prompts me to go ahead with my figuring and calculate the speed on the basis of Telemachus's return trip. The distance his ship covers from sandy Pylos until sunset is known, for it is, as we have already established, a distance of 65 kilometers, or 350 stades.

Once again, however, the time of departure, which we must know if we want to determine how long the trip took, can only be established by estimating the time elapsed since sunrise. I must, therefore, analyze very carefully the round trip by chariot between Pylos and Sparta.

On the trip over, Telemachus reaches Pylos at sunrise and spends part of the day with Nestor and his people. He has a chance to freshen up, and he spends quite some time eating and drinking with his hosts until they eventually offer him a chariot. He drives westward until evening and at sunset reaches Pharos, also called [Alphipheres,] which is located about midway along the Alpheios. He takes to the road again at sunrise and reaches Sparta with the setting sun.

The pattern is repeated on the drive back from Sparta. That is, Telemachus is driving along throughout the first day from sunrise to sunset and stays overnight at Pharos. He drives away from the city gates at dawn on the following day, heading toward sandy Pylos and anxious to board his ship without wasting any time.

Homer wishes to account for every minute of the time between the arrival of the chariot and the ship's departure. He tells us that Telemachus chooses not to report back to Nestor by driving up to the city, which seems to be at some distance from the harbor. Telemachus suspects that Nestor might be quite angry if he left without saying good-bye and accepting his parting gifts. He boards the ship just the same and orders his crew to be off immediately.

Here again we know the distance involved and can assign an approximate time to the trip. The trip by chariot between Pharos and

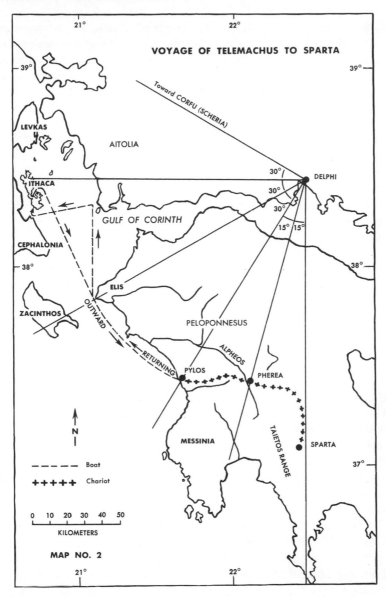

VOYAGE OF TELEMACHUS TO SPARTA

Toward CORFU (SCHERIA)

LEVKAS

AITOLIA

ITHACA

GULF OF CORINTH

CEPHALONIA

38°

ELIS

ZACINTHOS

OUTWARD

PELOPONNESUS

DELPHI

30°
30°
30°
15° 15°

38°

RETURNING

PYLOS

ALPHEOS

PHEREA

N

MESSINIA

TAIETOS RANGE

SPARTA

37°

- - - - Boat
+++++ Chariot

0 10 20 30 40 50
KILOMETERS

MAP NO. 2

21°   22°

Sparta takes a whole day in each direction, meaning by day the time between sunrise and sunset, that is, twelve hours. I can try to confirm this theory by checking the distances on land. The results are very vague because I do not know just which way the road went at the time. On the other hand, I do know that the actual route is far longer than the distance on the map as the crow flies, the proportions varying substantially with the terrain involved. It is easy to verify on any road map that sometimes we have to add 60 to 70 per cent to the distance as the crow flies to reach the actual number of kilometers to be covered in the average mountainous country. I choose to limit my reckoning to distances as the crow flies, or, more precisely, to their relationship. The one thing we know for certain is that in both directions the distance between Pharos and Sparta amounts to a 12-hour trek.

The map reveals that the lap between Pharos and sandy Pylos is shorter than the other by one-fourth, taking into account the distances and the terrain. This proportion of 100 to 75 for the two trips yields 50 and 37 kilometers, respectively, when applied to a straight line on the map. Whatever the actual distance covered, the important thing is this proportion of one to three-quarters, which enables us to conclude that on the last leg of the trip Telemachus has been driving for 9 hours.

Now, on this last part of the trip Telemachus crosses the gates of the fortress of Pharos not at sunrise but "as the rosy-fingered dawn" begins to show. This would mean that he left Pharos about one hour before sunrise, or he boarded his ship 8 hours after sunrise. That leaves him 4 hours of sailing until sundown. Since he covered 350 stades in 4 hours, we can conclude that 24 hours of sailing means a distance of exactly 2,100 stades. Thus this second calculation of speed, based on the return trip of the ship, confirms the results of the first one.

At this point a further question arises: What is the speed of the chariot? Will it be a likely one?

The route followed by Telemachus is broken down in two stages involving altogether 21 hours of driving to cover a distance of 87 kilometers as the crow flies, or about 150 kilometers on the road.

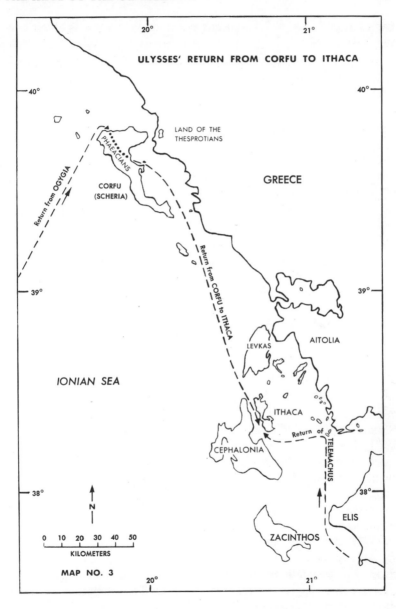

ULYSSES' RETURN FROM CORFU TO ITHACA

40°   40°

LAND OF THE
THESPROTIANS

PHAEACIANS

GREECE

CORFU
(SCHERIA)

Return from OGYGIA

Return from CORFU to ITHACA

39°   39°

AITOLIA

LEVKAS

IONIAN SEA

ITHACA

Return of

CEPHALONIA

TELEMACHUS

38°   38°

N

ELIS

0 10 20 30 40 50

KILOMETERS

ZACINTHOS

MAP NO. 3

20°   21°

The average speed of 7 kilometers per hour that we thus obtain is a quite likely one.

At this point I remembered the account of a third sea voyage between points that are easily identified on the map. I am speaking of the trip the Phaeacians made when they brought Ulysses from the island of Scheria (Corfu) to Ithaca. They put our hero ashore along the western coast, which we may suppose to be not too far from the southern end of the island since Ulysses can reach the swineherd on foot in a relatively short time. (See map No. 3.)

The last day on Corfu, Ulysses becomes very anxious to have the Phaeacians keep their promise and take him back to Ithaca. Homer emphasizes that he can hardly wait for the sunset to put to sea. Ulysses leaves at sunset and travels throughout the night. He sleeps aboard the ship and arrives "when the brightest of the stars" arises, the star that "comes to tell us that the dawn is near." I know from the analysis of Telemachus's voyage that setting sail at dawn means one hour before the rising of the sun. Applying this to Ulysses' case, he arrives one hour befor dawn, that is, two hours before sunrise. I am able to pin down the time spent at sea as 10 hours.

The map tells me that the middle of the western coast of Ithaca is at about 162 kilometers (or 875 stades) from the harbor of Corfu. The distance is covered in 10 hours. The average speed of 87.5 stades per hour is the same as we have established for the two other trips and amounts to 2,100 stades or 3.5 geographical degrees covered in 24 hours. Once more the speed figures confirm the previous calculations.

We have thus three separate trips the data of which are strictly independent of one another yet yield the same average speed for a ship. The coincidence is a quite troublesome one if it is, indeed, a coincidence. One may obviously wonder how precise the distance estimates are, but in this case the margin of error in the measurements is relatively small and has little effect on the final result.

At any rate, then, the three speed figures would remain very close. The calculations contain only one element that might appear arbitrary and subject to challenge; that is, the assumption we made about the morning hours. We have said that in every instance one hour goes by between the rising of the morning star and dawn, another hour between dawn and sunrise. We do know, however, that the ancients measured time by the hour or the twelfth part of the day, and it would seem to me even more arbitrary to adopt the fraction of an hour or a longer unit. Furthermore, any conceivable variation could affect the end result only to a comparatively small extent, and we can conclude that any eventual difference between the speeds established for the three trips would not be significant enough since the values involved are relatively low in the first place. I further conclude that in each of the three cases Homer intended to specify the average speed of the ships with some small possible deviation from the average. Running before the wind day and night for 24 hours, a ship sailing at this average speed can cover a distance that equals 3.5 geographical degrees.

The speed of ships is normally quoted in knots, a knot equaling one nautical mile per hour, or 1.850 kilometers per hour. Now, one geographical degree equals 60 nautical miles, and 3.5 degrees equal 210 nautical miles, which for 24 hours yields a speed of 8.7 knots. This is a rather brisk speed but quite normal when the sailing conditions are very favorable, which the story tells us is definitely the case.

Greek galleys are a favorite decorative theme on ancient pottery. The ships appear to be 80 to 100 feet long and rather narrow. Telemachus's craft had a crew of about twenty oarsmen, while the Phaeacian galley was manned by fifty-two. These vessels are fast pirate ships and not heavy transports. Taking this into account, we will find Homer's data for speed for the three quick trips quite acceptable, and I for one do not hesitate to adopt them as the first clue that shall help us decipher the message of the *Odyssey*.

If this clue is such an important one for decoding the meaning of Ulysses' voyage, the reader may wonder why it is not conveyed to us more explicitly and why we have to engage in every instance in a series of preliminary calculations in order to find it. Well, this very question brings us to the heart of the problem, which consists in finding out for what purpose the ancient Greeks used this epic poem and what reasons they had for concealing the actual message by such elaborate means.

I shall look into this question more closely and try to find an answer to it after I have established Ulysses' itinerary. At this moment I am more anxious to use the newly found key for opening the door to the adventure and following Ulysses' tracks than to worry about the reasons for their being camouflaged this way. So let us gather our maps of the Mediterranean and the Atlantic Ocean, our rulers and a compass, and set sail from Ithaca heading westward.

SUMMARY TABLE OF CALCULATIONS OF SAILING SPEED

VOYAGE OF TELEMACHUS	Distance in Km (as the crow flies)	Distance in Stades*	Time (hrs.)	Speed (stades)	Distance Covered in 24 hours (stades)
1st— going to Ithaca to Pylos (ship)	130	700	8	87.5	2,100
2nd— coming from					
Sparta to Pharos (chariot)	50		12		
Pharos to Pylos (chariot)	37		9	(daybreak departure)	
Pylos to western cape of Elia (ship)	65	350	4	87.5	2,100

VOYAGE OF ULYSSES					
Corfu to Ithaca (South) (ship)	162	875	10	87.5	2,100

*1 stade = 186 meters
600 stades = 1 degree

3.5 degrees

III. DISCOVERING THE ITINERARY OF ULYSSES

In Books 9 to 13, Ulysses tells the story of his voyage to the Phaeacians. They listen with astonishment and fascination.

As I mentioned earlier, I found one of the episodes of the trip unusual and somewhat unlikely. Ulysses' voyage as a whole shows a certain "logic"—a "way over" to the island of Ogygia, home of Calypso, and a "way back," which the poet narrates at the beginning of the poem. The unusual episode is the round trip between the island of Aeolia and the waters of Ithaca. I have concluded earlier that this quick trip is an imaginary one, that its story is told for the sole purpose of giving an accurate fix for Aeolia by referring it to Ithaca.

On leaving Aeolia, Ulysses is blessed by Zephyr, which brings him within sight of Ithaca in nine days of sailing. He runs ahead of the wind for nine days and nights. (See map no. 4.)

Now, one geographical degree equaling 111 kilometers, a speed of 3.5 degrees per 24 hours would yield a distance of 388 kilometers, or 3,492 kilometers in nine days.

I mark the island of Ithaca on the map of the Mediterranean as a first point of reference. Ithaca is situated at Greenwich longitude 21° east and latitude 38° north. I sail then westward at least as far as the Strait of Gibraltar, which is about 2,400 kilometers away.

The map shows three possible legs:

From Ithaca to the south of Sicily	550 kilometers
From Sicily to Cape Good	450
From Cape Good to Tangier	390
Total	2,390 kilometers

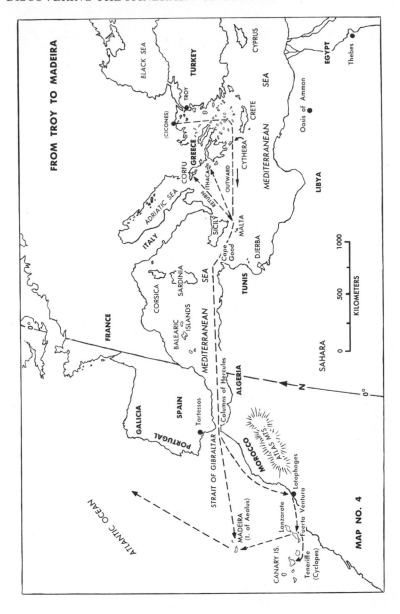

FROM TROY TO MADEIRA

MAP NO. 4

At this point I am at Tangier, situated at latitude 36° north and longitude 5.5° west.

I have 3,492 − 2,390 = 1,102 kilometers to account for. It so happens that the island of Madeira to the west and southwest of Tangier at latitude 33° north and longitude 17° west is at that distance almost to the kilometer. There is no other island in the whole area within a radius of several hundred kilometers. The figures are so precise that I cannot help wondering: Could all of this be mere coincidence?

Let us suppose that on three separate occasions I grossly over-calculated the ships' speed. What other island west of Ithaca will I find that satisfies all of the conditions? I would probably have to pull back to the Balearic Islands, or in any event to this side of Gibraltar, meaning that my previous calculations of speed were wrong by more than one-third. Since this is very unlikely, I must abandon the search in the Mediterranean and have a closer look at the results I have just obtained. The ominous cliffs of the island of Madeira in the middle of the Atlantic seem to fit well Ulysses' description: "a floating island: right round it was built a brazen wall unbreakable, and the rock ran up smooth and straight."

Other authors have been puzzled by this resemblance between the island of Madeira and Ulysses' description of the island of Aeolia. Theories identifying Madeira with the island of Aeolia have been published in the past, but without any additional supporting evidence.

I for one have no doubt about the identity of this important stopover, and I proceed to reconstruct the first stage of Ulysses' voyage that ends at this island of Aeolia. I am going to use my newly found key, the ships' speed, as an aid in estimating the distances involved.

For a second time, Ulysses travels for nine days when the storm blows him beyond Cythera. I can thus work here with the same distance as between the islands of Aeolia and Ithaca, that is, 3,492 kilometers.

We are leaving from a point situated at latitude 36° north and longitude 23° east (Cape Malea).

From this point, also, we can reach the Strait of Gibraltar in three legs:

From Cythera to the southern tip of Sicily	720 kilometers
From Sicily to Cape Good	450
From Cape Good to Tangier	1,390
Total	2,560 kilometers

If we subtract this distance from the total of 3,492 kilometers, we have 932 kilometers to go beyond the Strait of Gibraltar. Knowing that the country of the Lotus-eaters is a continent, I must look for it either toward Portugal to the northwest or along the Moroccan coast to the southwest. I prefer the second choice for the good reason that the prevailing Canary currents tend to divert the ships to the south as they emerge from the Strait of Gibraltar.

This distance of 932 kilometers will bring me ashore to the south of Agadir in the area between Ifni and the present border of Spanish Sahara (Cape Juby). This area today is desert land and seems like an unlikely place to bring forth the delicious lotus fruit that is supposed to make sailors forget their native country. Ulysses, however, does not actually speak here of a flourishing country or of abundant vegetation, whereas later on he spares no words in praising the fertility of the island of the archipelago where the Cyclôpes live. This "lotus" with its memory-blocking effects could be a drug well-known in Northern Africa, that is, the kif, or Indian hemp, that cured the sailors' homesickness and gave them the courage to leave the coast altogether and venture into the deep ocean. Assuredly, they had been sailing on the Atlantic Ocean ever since they left Gibraltar. They had a chance to get used to the long swell that is so different from the short waves of the Mediterranean Sea. Up to this point, however, they always kept the African coast in sight on their left. Now they must deliberately turn to the open waters of an unknown ocean. It is not so far-fetched to suppose that they welcomed whatever help they could find in the lotus.

Herodotus lists (Chapter IV, pp. 168–195) "the people that live along the Libyan coast." To appreciate his information, we must read "Lybia" as the ancients used the word. For them it meant the whole northern half of the African continent east of Egypt.

After Egypt come the Adormachides, then the Giligames, then
the Aslistes, then the Nasammons who live off their herds and in
the summer leave the shore and penetrate inland where they
harvest dates. They also eat locusts. After that come the Lotus-
eaters who live on nothing but lotus fruit, then the Machlyles . . .

The Lotus-eaters, therefore, were not an altogether imaginary
people. Placing them to the south of Morocco would agree well with
the list of Herodotus who starts with Egypt and continues westward.
The other four tribes could be placed in the area that goes today by
the name of Libya,that is, Tunisia, Algeria, and Morocco. As for the
Nasammons, the similarity is very striking between their way of life
as Herodotus describes it and the tribes of the Atlas range in
Morocco who also shift their herds with the seasons, harvest dates,
eat fried locusts . . .

Ulysses leaves the country of the Lotus-eaters sometime during
the day, and we know that at nightfall he reaches an uninhabited but
fertile island "neither too close nor too far" from the country of the
Cyclops.

Heading west from Cape Juby, a 120-kilometer crossing, or,
according to our key, about 8 hours of sailing, would take us directly
to the nearest island of the Canary archipelago, that is, Fuerteventura, or the neighboring Lanzarote.

That is where Ulysses and his companions spend the night in a
well-sheltered bay and are able to butcher some wild goats for food.
There exists, in fact, a harbor with safe mooring along the eastern
coast of Fuerteventura.

The country of the Cyclôpes, where grain, wine, and fruits of all
kinds grow spontaneously and in great abundance, can only be on
volcanic soil whose fertility is well known. As for the one-eyed
Cyclops "tall as a mountain," I have no reason to challenge former
commentators of the *Odyssey* who almost unanimously see in the
image a personification of a volcano. As it happens, there looms
before me to the west the great volcano of Tenerife, 3,700 meters
high. As Ulysses' fleet puts to sea from the land of the Cyclôpes,
Polyphemus the giant, blinded by Ulysses, throws rocks in the air
that fall on the sea around the ships. It would be difficult not to
think here of a volcanic eruption.

To sum up, we find numerous agreements from the strict geographical viewpoint between Homer's text and the topography of the Canary archipelago: the distance from the African continent; a large, active volcano; nearby, a flatter island covered with dense vegetation and offering shelter for the ships; the fertile volcanic soil affording, according to Ulysses, tremendous possibilities for colonization. Let us remember here that the Canary Islands have long been called the "Islands of Fortune" because of this very fertility of their soil.

I discover, however, another puzzling coincidence, this time an ethnographic one. Ulysses reports that the people on these islands live in caves, and since they know nothing about seafaring, some of the available land, such as the nearby island where Ulysses first puts to shore, remains unoccupied. We might also point out incidentally that the account leaves no doubt as to the nature of the area, that is, a group of islands, or an archipelago.

When the Norman navigator Jean de Béthencourt discovered the Canary Islands in 1402, he found there a white indigenous population, the Guanches. We do not know to this day where these people originally came from. He tells us that the natives are cave-dwellers, and he points out in his report that they populate only some of the islands.

We know that the Guanches had no ships. It is very tempting, indeed, to compare these two discoveries, which seem to have so much in common. Could the life of these people, isolated in the ocean, have remained unchanged for two and a half thousand years? In any event, the possibility could not be ruled out altogether.

I am anticipating the reader's question. How did these people ever come to these islands in the first place if we reject the theory of spontaneous generation on the one hand, and, on the other, if we refuse to believe that the art of seafaring could be forgotten by a people that had once known it? How do we explain the presence of these people on the islands in the first place?

We can do little else than theorize on this point. We may think that the Canary archipelago is what is left of a larger chunk of land once attached to the African continent. Its collapsing into the ocean could account for the origin of the legend of Atlantis.

Greek mythology seems to be referring to some prehistoric cata-
strophe when it speaks of Atlas's sinking into the sea. It is interesting
to note that the Atlas range, not too far from the area, should have
kept its name since antiquity.

We should pursue our own appointed round, though, and let
others worry about developing this theory. Ulysses is not going to
wait for us. There he is with his fleet of twelve ships, rowing away
without stopping until he reaches the island of Aeolia. At a latitude
of 4° toward the north, along the meridian located at 17° west, we
find the island of Madeira. Ulysses travels about 450 kilometers on a
northerly course. One may wonder how it was possible in that era to
find an island lost in the ocean when the ships were at the mercy of
the winds and strange currents.

We know today that the Phoenicians used the polar star as a
guide in navigation. In Ulysses' case, therefore, it was easy enough to
stay on course. Moreover, the island of Madeira is more than 30
kilometers long. We can add at least that much on both ends since
the island is visible from afar. The weather is generally clear in the
area, and the island rises rather high on the horizon. We might also
suppose that the fleet of Ulysses is not traveling in a close formation
but is spread out to cover a wider sector. If we take all of this into
account, a simple reckoning will show that the ships would have had
to be at least 15 degrees off a due-north course to miss Madeira and
sail by without sighting it. And if that had been the case, the chief
navigator would have soon discovered the error as sailing time was
getting longer than it was supposed to. He would then have referred
to his "Jacob's stick," a rather primitive instrument designed to
calculate the approximate height of a star over the horizon (in our
case the polar star) and obtain a fix on the latitude. The polar star is
located on the zenith, that is, at 90 degrees above if we view it from
the North Pole, or on the horizon if we are at the equator.

Obtaining a longitudinal fix calls for more complex sightings, and
we do not know today what method the ancients could have used,
short of following the coastline, to reach an even remotely valid
reading once they were out of sight of the coast.

Since the navigator was able to figure his latitude, he could tell if
he had reached the latitude of his destination, such as an island. In

that case, he would change course by 90 degrees and run along a parallel until he found what he was looking for. If Ulysses used this technique to reach again the Mediterranean from a point in the Atlantic Ocean, his most likely route would be to follow a due north-south bearing until he reached the latitude of Gibraltar (36°), then steer a due-east course leading him inevitably into the strait.

Now, it is relatively easy to find a strait when the navigator is guided for many miles by two narrowing coastlines. Finding an island on the open sea is another matter. It is therefore safe to say that the return trip of Ulysses raises no particular problems, in the supposition that he follows due bearings, first south, then east.

This speculating on ancient methods of navigation prompts me to think again of Ulysses' homecoming after he leaves the goddess Calypso. I have some precise information: 17 days of navigation, day and night, on a north-south bearing at the start. I shall try to apply my key to this new leg of the trip.

Since I am now at Madeira, this leg of the homeward trip is on the Atlantic. If Ulysses uses the technique described above, he must lose latitude until he reaches 36° north, at the level of the Strait of Gibraltar, and then steer a west-east course.

Since Madeira is at longitude 17° west, I count 9 days for the trip from Madeira to Ithaca. I shall attempt to reach a distance equaling 9 days of sailing by following the 36th parallel from longitude 17°, which is the meridian of Madeira, to the island of Scheria which Ulysses is heading for. (See map. No. 4.)

From point P to Tangier	1,050 kilometers
From Tangier to Cape Good	1,390
From Cape Good to the south of Sicily	450
From Sicily to Corfu	580
Total	3,470 kilometers

Nine days of sailing add up to 388 × 9 = 3,492 kilometers, 22 kilometers more than the above total. Ulysses must evidently be running 9 days on a west-east course along the 36th parallel, taking off from the meridian of Madeira. Since the homeward trip lasted 17 days, we have a balance of 8 days for the north-south leg along the meridian of Madeira. Ulysses covers the length of 3.5° of latitude per

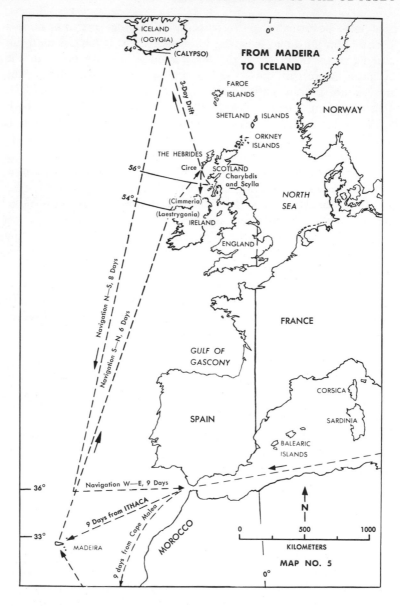

day, or 28° in 8 days on his north-south course. Now, 28° to the north of the 36th parallel yields latitude 28 + 36 = 64° north. (See map. No. 5.)

In other words, Ulysses takes off on his homeward trip from a point at latitude 64° north and longitude 17° west. These coordinates effectively cross along the shoreline on an island, that is, in the middle of the southeast coast of Iceland. I must confess that I was not altogether surprised by these results. Applying my key, the speed of the ships, to the 17-day homeward trip of Ulysses merely confirmed the conclusions that other data made me anticipate. I am now ready to sum up the whole situation.

This sector of the coastline defined by the two coordinates meets all of the five conditions dictated by Homer's text.

1. The area is located exactly to the northwest of Mount Olympus along a straight line drawn from the top of Mt. Olympus across the highest peak of Pieria (Flight of Hermes).

2. From this location at latitude 64°, one can see the Great Bear and the Pleiades all night. Aries barely touches the ocean while the other constellations sink below the horizon with every rotation of the earth.

3. To return to Greece, Ulysses must first steer a southerly course. A sky chart of that century would show us that during fall nights the Great Bear was always to the left, that is, to the east. At midnight the Pleiades were directly to the south, and Ulysses was facing them as he held the helm.

4. On the basis of the speed figures we have established for the trips on the Mediterranean, the distance to Greece equals 17 days of constant day-and-night sailing.

5. The point we have located is along the coast of an island.

This multiple evidence should be convincing enough, yet I am not completely satisfied.

There remains, in fact, one hazy detail. Homer draws for us a picture of Calypso's garden and the fruit trees and flowers. The names do not fit the climate of Iceland as we know it today. Neither do I think that one could actually find there the kind of pine forests that supplied the timber for Ulysses' craft. On the other hand, the fall season is still young, yet there is a fire burning in Calypso's cave, which must be at sea level since the beach where Ulysses is sitting is quite close. All of this would indicate that the area is far up to the north.

My first reaction is to discount Homer's description either as a routine poetic tribute to the goddess Calypso or as an exaggeration typical of the returning sailor who tells the folks at home about the enchanting lands he discovered. As I reread the passage, however, I find several other possible explanations.

One has to do with climatic evolution. We know today that a climate may change over a period of several thousand years. These variations may affect the mean temperature or the level of humidity. Three thousand years, however, are hardly a long enough period to account for a climatic change as radical as in our case.

The second explanation takes into account the strong volcanic activity we find on Iceland. The year-round flow of hot springs could create locally tempered subclimates. Homer himself lends support to this theory when he speaks of "fountains that flow in four different directions," with the apparent intention of explaining the fertility of the land. He does not use the word "spring." An ordinary spring would have to originate at midslope, or at the foot of an elevation, and would flow downhill. In our case, the word "fountain" is used, implying a major stream. Water flows in all directions only if it originates at the top of a knoll. This is characteristic of Iceland's volcanic hot springs where certain components dissolved in the water are deposited around the point from which it spouts and eventually build up into a mound around the opening.

A third explanation: the vocabulary used by Ulysses. The names of the plants that make up the garden are borrowed from Mediterranean nomenclature. Sailors, in fact, do not normally qualify as expert botanists. Arriving at a new island and in contact with unknown plants that resemble certain species of their home country, the sailors would spontaneously designate the new plants by the only words they knew, or else they would not be understood later by the people at home.

After describing a plant the first time as "a type of vine" or "a kind of fig tree," the narrator tends to simplify his style and eventually says just "vine" or "fig tree."

In other words, I would not think it too important that northern plants go here by Mediterranean names. Nor should one jump to the conclusion that the country thus characterized must be Corsica or Sicily.

A sailor, on the other hand, makes no mistake when he identifies the wind pushing his ship or the movement of the stars.

After playing "devil's advocate," I can say in conclusion: "*I believe in Iceland.*" Following Hermes or Ulysses on the initial voyage just as on the return one, too many coincidences point to that island for me to doubt that Iceland was the last stop of that legendary trip.

Now I know two essential points of Ulysses' trip: an intermediate stage, the island of Madeira, and the final destination, Iceland. I also know that he reached Madeira from Greece by hugging the African coast after passing through the Strait of Gibraltar and touching at the Canaries.

The method followed until now was rather simple. All I had to do was to combine my first key, the speed of the ship, with the data of my chart on navigation time and the direction. The next step was simply to see if the places thus identified on the map fit all other topographical information in the text: latitude, climate, landscape, etc.

The results obtained so far by this method have been very encouraging. I am impatient, then, to leave the island of Madeira in order to find out how and by what route Ulysses arrived at Iceland. I am very anxious to be able to identify the islands and countries visited, and, especially, to rediscover the whirlpool of Charybdis and the cave of Scylla.

After leaving the island of Aeolia, that is, Madeira, Ulysses and his war fleet sail on for 6 days. They must be headed north, since, as we have seen, the area they reach is located at a high latitude where the days are longer.

Our key enables us to conclude that following a due-north course along the meridian of Madeira, or longitude 17° west, the ships take six days to cover six times 3.5°, that is, to reach latitude 21°.

Madeira is located on the 33rd parallel, and Ulysses' fleet reaches the latitude 33° + 21° = 54° north.

The only land in that latitude in an approximate northerly direction from Madeira is Ireland, more exactly the west coast of Ireland in County Connaught between Galway and the island of Achill—an interesting name to mark our itinerary.

That region seems to fit well the description of the famous port of Lamos in the land of Telepylos inhabited by the Laestrygonians. We are told of a humid country abounding in forest and springs and of a deeply indented rocky coastline providing good natural harbors. Ulysses' fleet finds itself entering a harbor that is practically closed off from the sea. It is surrounded by precipitous cliffs from which rocks are thrown at ships that have taken refuge deep inside the port. These natural harbors, steep-walled valleys invaded by the sea, are typical of the primary (hercynian) mountain formations in Brittany, Wales, Ireland, Scotland.

The port Ulysses mentions must have been well-known since he uses the word "famous," that is, "whose renown has reached abroad." Ulysses' ship is the only one to escape the general massacre. At this point we find few hints enabling us to trace the next stage. No sailing days are given, only a simple outline of direction: "we sail ahead . . . ", meaning perhaps the same northerly course, which would bring Ulysses near the archipelago of the Hebrides.

Ulysses admits that he is lost in the fog and cannot see the sun even in broad daylight. He does not find his bearings until he reaches Aea, the island of Circe.

Is this the southermost island of the Hebrides?

Or is it one of the islands bordering the Scottish coast farther east? Or farther north, toward the Orcades? Or the Shetlands?

I must confess that in using the maps of the British Isles I let my imagination roam for a long time in these parts. I am forced to surrender to the evidence that this course will lead me nowhere except into pure speculation and unsupported hypothesizing, something that I have been able to avoid up to now.

However, an idea occurs to me as I now reread my original outline of directions and time spans, which I could have attempted sooner. Instead of following Ulysses from Madeira in the chronological order of events, why not leave from Iceland, the second solid point, and unravel the story backward? This second approach is going to prove much more effective when I try it. I abandon, then, for a while my fumbling search for Circe's island, and I climb in latitude to the banks of Iceland at latitude 64° north and longitude 16° east, near the goddess Calypso's cave. Here we spot Ulysses for the first time, seated on the shore, despairing of ever seeing his faraway Ithaca again.

How he reached here and where he came from still must be explained. Ulysses, clinging to his ship without any mast and unable to steer, arrives at this coast after nine days adrift.

Here we find a new mystery. What do nine days adrift in such circumstances mean in terms of distance on the map?

This period begins to run at the moment when Ulysses, aboard the wreckage of his ship, clears the dangers of Charybdis and Scylla for the second time, propelled by Notus, in a south-north direction.

Hence, it is the very position of Charybdis and Scylla that I hope to determine by converting, if I can, the 9 days adrift into terms of exact distance and direction.

The problem seems, *a priori*, an insoluble one, and I am ready to give up this hopelessly difficult task.

The second approach with Iceland as a start seems at first even more fruitless than the other one I have tried.

But then I think it over and decide that Homer should be trusted. Since the text has so far supplied me, often at quite unexpected places, with the information I needed, a second key is bound to turn up sooner or later. I reread once more the passage referring to those nine days adrift. Then I continue to the point where Ulysses, back in Ithaca, pretends to be a Cretan sailor because he does not want to be recognized by Eumaeus the swineherd. He tells of an imaginary trip to Egypt, Phoenicia, and Crete. The pseudo-Ulysses, on his way back from Egypt to Libya approaches Crete only to be pushed back toward the south by Boreas. A storm breaks at the precise moment when he is far enough from Crete to be "out of sight of land." I am suddenly alerted, for the following two lines are the same as Homer has used to describe the ship struck by lightning at the departure from the island of Thrinacia.

> Zeus thundered and lightened together and struck the ship; her timbers all shivered at the stroke, and the place was filled with sulphur. All on board were cast into the sea. They were carried over the black water bobbing about on the waves like so many black crows; it was God's will that they should never see home again . . . nine days I drifted; on the tenth . . .

It seemed immediately evident to me that there was a reference here intended to stimulate in our mind an association between the two events.

We have here a period of nine days adrift in the Mediterranean that begins in the same conditions as the real voyage. I am at once certain that I found the second key to Homer's tale. Once more he uses the method of transferring the real events to the Mediterranean in order to give the distance covered during those 9 days and perhaps even the direction followed.

I must leave for a while the mists of Iceland and place myself in the Mediterranean sunshine in order to discover this new key before I continue the adventure.

I will try first to locate the shipwreck site.

I intend to calculate the coordinates of the departure and arrival points of those 9 days adrift. From the coordinates, I will figure the distance covered in latitude and longitude. Then, returning to my point of arrival in Iceland in the real voyage, I will subtract from the coordinates of this point the distances covered in longitude and latitude in order to determine the coordinates of the departure point of the nine days adrift.

In theory, this calculation seems rather simple, for it amounts to transposing a triangle D. A. H. (departure point, arrival point, and point H crossing the meridian line of the arrival point with the parallel of the departure point). All I have to do is to apply point D of the triangle to the presumed site of Calypso's cave in Iceland, that is, latitude 64° north and longitude 16° east, in order to determine point A, or the site of Charybdis and Scylla.

But let us listen more attentively to Ulysses' tale:

I stayed with him (in Phoenicia) for a full year . . . he took me on board for a voyage to Lybia . . . The ship ran before a fair wind across the open sea to the windward of Crete . . . When we had left Crete behind and were out of sight of land, only sea and sky to be seen, Cronion brought a black cloud over the ship, and the sea grew dark beneath it.

There follows, then, the description of the shipwreck.

It is clear, then, that the ship, coming from Phoenicia, sails by the eastern end of Crete and is presently south of the island since the Boreas wind that pushes it toward the south, or Libya, passes over Crete.

Mr. Harrell Courtes in *Les Fils de Minos* says this about the ancient Cretan ports: "In the south of the island trading took place by way of Trypitis at the foot of the Asterussa mountains." This port is indeed the first encountered on the southern coast as one comes from the east, that is from Phoenicia. Sailing from there toward Libya, a ship would follow an approximate north-south bearing along the meridian at longitude 26° east. At what latitude along that meridian did the shipwreck occur? The problem is to figure from what distance at sea the mountains, which rise to about 2,500 meters, would no longer be visible, allowing for the curvature of the earth and supposing perfect visibility. The calculation results in a distance of about 100 nautical miles, or a little less than 2 latitudinal degrees. The latitude of the southern coast of Crete being 35°, the ship, when it meets destruction, has probably cleared the 33rd parallel. At the 32nd parallel, it would be too close to the African coast. The shipwreck, therefore, could only have taken place between these two latitudes. I allow the following mean coordinates for the shipwreck site where the nine-day drifting started:

Latitude 32.5° north
Longitude 26° east

Nine days I drifted; on the tenth dark night I was thrown up by a great wave on the Thesprotian shore . . . There I heard of Ulysses. The king said he had entertained him as a guest . . . The

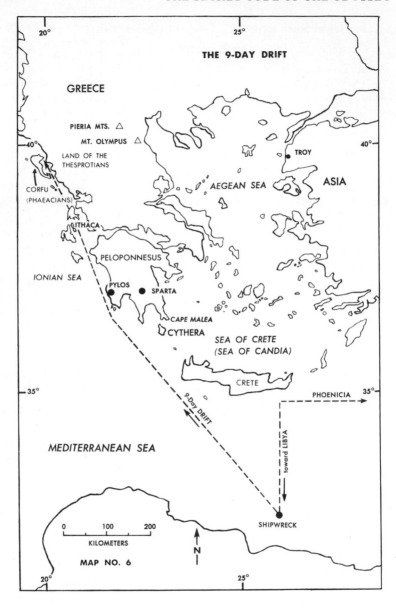

THE 9-DAY DRIFT

GREECE

PIERIA MTS. △

MT. OLYMPUS △

LAND OF THE
THESPROTIANS

CORFU
(PHAEACIANS)

ITHACA

AEGEAN SEA   ASIA

TROY

PELOPONNESUS

IONIAN SEA

PYLOS   SPARTA

CAPE MALEA
CYTHERA

SEA OF CRETE
(SEA OF CANDIA)

9-Day DRIFT

CRETE

PHOENICIA

toward LIBYA

MEDITERRANEAN SEA

0   100   200

KILOMETERS

N

MAP NO. 6

SHIPWRECK

king said he had gone to Dodona that he might learn the will of Zeus from the great oak, and find out how he ought to return to Ithaca after his long absence.

The land of the Thesprotians is located in the ancient province of Ephyra opposite Corfu in the southern part of present Albania.

The shrine of Dodona is in fact located in that region. For a landing site, we can reasonably choose a spot situated at the latitude of Olympus, the 40th parallel. So for an arrival point we have the following coordinates:

Latitude 40° north
Longitude 20° east

By referring these data to the coordinates of the shipwreck site, I find that the nine-day drifting covered latitude $40° - 32.5° = 7.5°$ and longitude $26° - 20° = 6°$ east. Now, a degree of longitude at latitude 32.5° represents a distance of 95 kilometers. The drift toward the west was the $95 \times 6 = 570$ kilometers. I am going to apply these two essential data to the Atlantic trip, supposing that the two nine-day drifts are identical in latitude and longitude, that is:

7.5 degrees in latitude
570 kilometers in longitude

As the arrival point at Iceland is located under latitude 64°, the departure point would be located above latitude $64° - 7.5° = 56.5°$. We have thus a first coordinate for the rocks of Charybdis and Scylla.

For the longitude, the arrival point is located at 16° west of Greenwich. I descend 7.5° toward the south along this meridian. From there I must count 570 kilometers toward the east to find the departure point.

How many longitudinal degrees do 570 kilometers amount to along the 56.5° parallel?

It is easily verified on a map that at this latitude a degree east or west equals 60 kilometers. Hence, the 570 kilometers represent exactly 9.5 degrees of distance toward the east.

In order to get the longitude of Charybdis and Scylla, we must only subtract 9.5 degrees from 16 degrees to get 6.5 degrees west of Greenwich.

To sum up, the coordinates of the rocks of Charybdis and Scylla would be, according to this calculation:

Latitude 56.5° north
Longitude 6.5° west

Now that these figures appear on paper, I hurry to open the atlas at the page on the British Isles to locate this point. Look at the map with me and trace the two lines of the coordinates, a vertical line at 6.5° west and a horizontal line at latitude 56.5°. You will find a point located in Scotland, off the western coast in the neighborhood of the isle of Coll. In fact, between that island and the isle of Mull, a kind of north-south canal joins the Sea of the Hebrides with the north canal, which is the entrance to the Irish Sea. Examining on a larger scale map the islands that are located around this point, I notice close by two small islets, then another that is called the isle of Staffa. Now open the geographical section of any dictionary and what you read will surprise you. From Staffa you will be told to refer to Fingal (cave of . . .), where you read: "Famous Scottish cave on the island of Staffa, 69 meters long by 20 meters high, the nave of which is supported by basaltic columned walls. The sea enters through an opening of 13 meters and splashes against the back of this musical cavern." (*Petit Larousse*, 270th edition).

You will also learn that this peculiarity inspired the composer Mendelssohn to give the title "Fingal's Cave" to one of his works.

Remember now Ulysses' description relating to Scylla's cave. "In the side of the cliff there is a dark gloomy cave, facing the west . . . , so high that the strongest man could not reach it with an arrow from the ship . . . her (Scylla's) voice is no louder than a puppy dog new-born . . ." Circe had already pointed out to Ulysses: "the stone is smooth as if it had been polished."

The rock of Staffa is formed precisely by basalt columns that plunge vertically into the sea. The spectacle of these orderly rocks, smooth like columns, was indeed likely to strike a sailor's imagination and to suggest that it had been cut and polished. The description of the cave, with its opening level with the sea, its bluish depths, the roaring that issues from it that could only come from a frightful

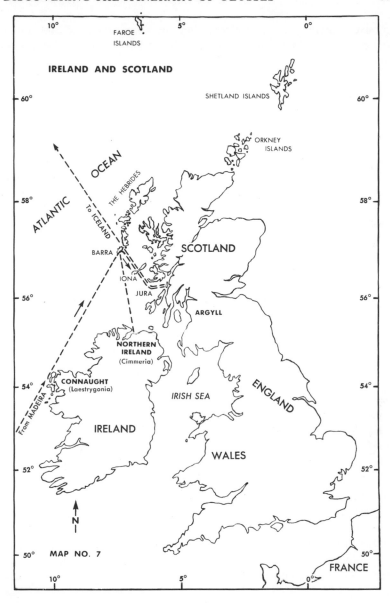

MAP NO. 7

monster spying on the sailors from the deep recess of his cavern, points to near-perfect agreement between the topography of the place and Homer's text.

In regard to Scylla's cave, there does not seem to exist anywhere, either in the Mediterranean or in the Atlantic, a cave that meets so perfectly the requirements of the text.

As for the whirlpool of Charybdis, I would place it below a second rock very near the first. The whole western coast of Scotland is dented with islands and inlets. The tide, forcing its way into the narrow passages between the islands and the coast, creates violent coastal currents and recurring whirlpools every 6 hours—still another phenomenon to strike a Mediterranean sailor's imagination as he passes through these parts for the first time.

Circe told Ulysses: "Charybdis underneath (the other cliff) swallows down the black water. Three times a day she spouts it out, three times a day she swallows it down." We know that the phenomenon is brought about by the tide and must occur every six hours. Since the event occurs "three times a day," a day covers eighteen hours. The night at that latitude lasts only six hours, or one-fourth of twenty-four hours. We are told that Ulysses sails during "the long days," which can be interpreted as an indication of season, probably close to the June solstice.

These basic data prompted me to calculate the possible latitude of a place where a night at the end of June lasted six hours.

I have mentioned above that our calculations would place the latitude of Charybdis in the area of the 57th parallel—still another confirmation of Charybdis' and Scylla's site. Can we still be skeptical after these initial conclusions? No doubt, all this could theoretically be the result of chance. In that case, though, one would have to honestly calculate the degree of probability that unites so many coincidences.

Personally, this discovery of Fingal's Cave assures me beyond a doubt that I am on the right track to finding Ulysses' true itinerary.

Only the famous strait between the two rocks and the periodic whirlpool remain now to be located on the map.

Still going backward in time, I return now to Ulysses' voyage after leaving Charybdis and Scylla. Ulysses, hanging on to the wreckage of his ship, was pushed all night by the south wind (Notus) and arrived at Charybdis at sunrise. In summer, the night is short at that latitude, and the drifting time must not have been much more than seven hours. Knowing that he covered an average of a little more than 100 kilometers a day drifting from Charybdis to the island of Ogygia, I must place the shipwreck site about 30 kilometers south of the island of Staffa, that is, between the islands of Mull and Islay. The ship was heading south or southwest since Ulysses says that he was forced by the south wind to remain at the island of Thrinacia for a month. He was waiting for the north wind, then, to set sail. Since he was returning home, only the north wind would serve his purpose. Thrinacia is located north of this point but very near Scylla's cave, for Ulysses specifies that he arrives at that island very soon after the Charybdis and Scylla episode.

The southern tip of the island of Mull seems to fulfill these two conditions.

Mull would then be the island of Thrinacia, or Trident. Indeed, its three tips facing west do resemble a trident.

Since the south wind pushed Ulysses past Charybdis and Scylla a second time, one can gather that he approached the rocks the first time from a point either to the north of them or northwest or northeast. Now he was coming from Aea where Circe lives.

If that island had been due north of the rocks, Ulysses would have already cleared the dangers of Charybdis and Scylla when, heading for the country of the Cimmerians, he steered due south, pushed by the north wind. Circe's island, consequently, cannot be located on the same meridian with those famous rocks.

Likewise, the map shows that a localization to the northeast must be eliminated, for the indentation of the Scottish coast does not permit the crossing of the ocean in a north-south direction. Only the Orcades and the Shetlands north of Scotland have an open sea south of them; but their distance in relation to Charybdis and Scylla forces me to eliminate them.

In fact, Ulysses leaves Circe in the morning and reaches the island of Thrinacia by evening.

Under these conditions, one could only locate Circe's island in a northwest direction. Furthermore, this island is not very large, for Ulysses sees from his mountain vantage point that the sea circles it like a crown. Hence, the island of Barra, the most southerly of the Hebrides, holds my attention. Given these circumstances, the island of the Sirens, which Ulysses must skirt before reaching the rocks, could be the island of Tiree or Coll island located on the line that runs from Barra south to the rocks of Staffa.

Moreover, south of Barra, the sea is unobstructed all the way to the northern coast of Ireland, and the distance to be covered along a north-south axis closely approximates 185 kilometers. In fact, Ulysses sails one day from sunrise to sunset in order to return to the Cimmerians' country. That is about half the distance he usually covers in twenty-four hours (about 385 kilometers according to the adopted scale).

The foggy land of the Cimmerians, where the inhabitants do not see the sun, could well be Northern Ireland. This localization is satisfactory if we remember that Ireland holds the European record for number of foggy days per year.

Ulysses sails up the river Oceanos, carried by the current for a short distance. On the way back, he lets himself be carried to the open sea.

This is a fit description of these Irish rivers whose mouth, a valley invaded by the sea as in Brittany, is sensitive to tidal movements.

Now, in our particular case, the river located at the required distance south of the island of Barra is the Foyle River. Upstream from Londonderry, it is actually formed by the meeting of two rivers, as Ulysses describes. The relative positions of Barra and of North Ireland are perfectly in accord with Ulysses' tale and with that of Circe; she herself suggests his route on the eve of his departure. Still retracing Ulysses' voyage in time, I must next connect that episode with his departure from the island of Aeolia, and locate his unlucky adventures in the land of the Laestrygonians.

A line joining Madeira (isle of Aeolia) to Barra cuts the west coast of Ireland at County Connaught, that is, at the height of the

54th parallel. Now, I had already figured that Ulysses, sailing for 6 days and nights after leaving the island of Aeolia, covered a distance equal to 3.5 degrees in 24 hours, or 21 degrees in 6 days. The island of Madeira is located exactly on the thirty-third parallel. After covering 21 degrees in a northerly direction, Ulysses then reached latitude 54°. No need to look any farther for the country of Telepylos, inhabited by the fierce Laestrygonians. A much closer examination of the coast should yield the site of the deep and "famous" port of Lamos, "with precipitous cliffs running all around. At the mouth are two headlands projecting front to front, and the entry is narrow."

The water level, however, has heightened since that period, very noticeably, for example, in Brittany, and could have modified the appearance of the sites by enlarging the bays and passages.

Ulysses' descriptions of the Laestrygonians' country apply perfectly to this region of Ireland: a country of mountains and indented coasts, rocks falling vertically into the ocean, and deep ports well sheltered from the surge of the open sea. "There were no waves rising inside, large or small." The men Ulysses sends ashore to investigate find "a levelled road which was used by carts to carry down wood from the hills to the city."

The circle is now complete, and we are ready to make the first serious attempt at sketching Ulysses' itinerary in its general features. From Greece, Ulysses sails west beyond Gibraltar. Then, skirting the coast of Africa, he arrives at "a continent," the land of the Lotus-eaters in southern Morocco. The same day, he sets sail again; by evening he reaches one of the Canary Islands, the one opposite the Cyclôpes' land, that is, the volcano of Tenerife. After an expedition to this island, he sails toward Medeira (Aeolia), which he reaches from the southeast. The fictitious trip from Madeira to Ithaca only serves to locate the island of Aeolia in relation to Greece, that is, nine days of sailing west.

Ulysses, scudding north, reaches the west coast of Ireland at the 54th parallel. There he finds the "lofty stronghold of Lamos" at Telepylos where he loses all the ships except his own. Nevertheless, he continues "onward" still on course and reaches the island of Barra, the most southerly of the Hebrides, where he finds a strategic position for wintering and for exploring the neighboring islands.

The following year, in June, "during the long days," he sails due south until he reaches the north coast of Ireland at the mouth of the Foyle River. This is the foggy land of the Cimmerians. Carried along by the rising tide, he goes upstream to a point where two rivers meet. He turns back toward the evening, riding the river Oceanos downstream. A night's journey brings him back to his base at Barra. The next day, he sets sail again in a southeast direction toward the island of Mull. On his way, he passes Coll, or Tiree, home of the Sirens, followed immediately by the rocks of Charybdis and Scylla. The deep cave on the island of Staffa and the mumurings coming from it strike his imagination. The tall, smooth columns of basalt impress him, and he notices that it is impossible to climb them.

He also notices that the whirlpool of Charybdis comes alive three times a day, that is, once every six hours, for at that latitude the day lasts eighteen hours at the time of the summer solstice.

He quickly arrives at the southern part of the island of Mull where he is held up by the south and east winds.

Apparently, Ulysses wants to inform us that after leaving Thrinacia, where the crew slaughtered the cattle of Helios, he needed a north wind to continue his homeward trip. Shortly after his departure, the ship is struck by lightning. After a night's drifting, a strong south wind carries Ulysses once more past Charybdis and Scylla.

A constant south or southeast wind then pushes him for nine days and nights toward the southeast coast of Iceland at latitude 64° north and about longitude 16° west. We are in faraway Ogygia, home of Calypso.

Ulysses remains for 7 years on that island. After putting together a vessel, he sets sail at the end of summer. He is careful to remark that in that country the entire constellation of the Great Bear remains visible throughout the night. Sailing in a southerly direction, he reaches latitude 36° north, or the height of the Strait of Gibraltar. Nine days of sailing east along this parallel brings him back to Greece at the island of Corfu—seventeen days all told since leaving Iceland. Thanks to the help of the Phaeacians, he returns in one night from Corfu to Ithaca.

There we have the general outline of the itinerary such as it appeared to me after a study of the text and the maps. I am convinced that the likelihood of this hypothesis and the essential agreement between Homer's text and the distances as we plotted them on the map create the best hopes for this proposed itinerary to be confirmed by an actual repetition of the voyage. But even if I do obtain, as I hope I will, a verification by physical scouting of the terrain, I must state that the text alone was not a sufficient tool in establishing the itinerary. Only by repeated examination of the maps and the relative positions of the islands was I able to deduce and crosscheck to eliminate the unlikely variants, and to select the only course that would fit the text.

So far as we know, there were no exact maps in Homer's time. For that reason, although the itinerary we discovered shows the voyage to be a real one, that does not mean necessarily that Ulysses' contemporaries were able to find the same route by using the text. Actually, in the present state of my analysis, I would not know which way to steer the ship when there is no reference to the direction of the wind. That point is very important. If the text alone is not enough to follow the itinerary, the meaning of the *Odyssey* is very different from my initial hypothesis. In that case, this travel story is the account of an unusual adventure centered around the personality of Ulysses. Its purpose is to praise and transmit to posterity the record of his great qualities as a navigator, his courage, and his cunning. The voyage, then, is an accompaniment to the main theme of the adventure; ports visited and directions followed have only an incidental meaning providing a backdrop against which the hero's deeds can be limelighted.

If, on the other hand, the text alone sufficed to retrace the itinerary through the precise information it supplies on course and distance, then the meaning of the *Odyssey* is completely different. In that case, we have the exact description of a maritime route disguised as a personal adventure clocked in mythology and intelligible only to the initiated. Then, the true theme of the *Odyssey* is no longer Ulysses' adventures but the mystery of a jealously guarded secret accessible only to the Achaeans' descendants.

If, as I believe, the *Odyssey's* text has a meaning for the Achaean sailors, if it is truly a message meant for them, then certain facts have escaped me.

Each time the wind is not indicated, there must exist a code that suggests the course to take.

The code is now clear enough for the distances covered. Each time that the distance is more than a day's sailing, it is expressed by navigation days or by days of drifting.

By contrast, the direction suggested by the name of the wind— Boreas, Notus, Zephyr, or Eurus—is mentioned in only half the instances, and only to indicate the cardinal points. I am naturally led to think that in the other cases there exists in the text a code that indicated to the Achaeans the course to steer.

IV. THE SIGNS OF THE ZODIAC

At the same time as I was pondering these problems, trying to identify the words Ulysses used to indicate spatial directions, a new book entitled *Sacred Geography of the Greek World* was published by Jean Richer. I soon realized that his theory would shed new light on the *Odyssey*.

He claims, in fact, that from the earliest times of Greek history a relationship existed between spatial directions and the signs of the zodiac. In more general terms, the map of the heavens and the constellations was projected on the earth, and once a central point was agreed upon, the location of a city or region could be determined by the zodiacal sign located in the same direction on a stellar map. Because of its projection on earth, the zodiacal wheel used to indicate bearings in an inverted order. The 12 signs fixed the boundaries of twelve 30-degree sectors, or 12 directions in space, each 30 degrees wide.

Going clockwise, the signs are numbered from 1 to 12 like the hours on a dial plate, with the twelfth hour pointing north:

For Greece, the center of this system was the temple of Delphi, the focal site of Greek religion and the oracles. The [author] arrived at this conclusion after analysis of signs on coins from the main Greek cities and on sculptures appearing on temple pediments. The coincidences are really disturbing. It seems evident that certain places were chosen as centers of a system of polar coordinates, that is, of lines radiating from one point. These lines probably served the priests as guidelines for orienting Greek expansion, locating a city or a temple, and deciding which gods should be honored there, depending on the city's position on the zodiacal wheel.

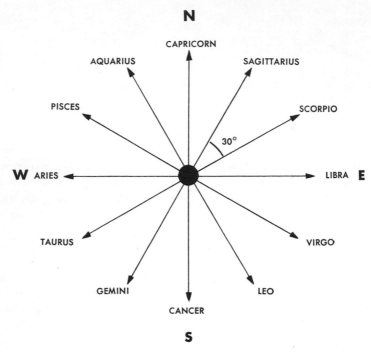

Three centers probably existed: Delphi and Delos in Greece, and Sardis in Asia Minor. The second, Delos, is on the meridian of Ammonium in Egypt, famous for its temple dedicated to the Egyptian god Amon.

This place, the present oasis of Siwa, seems to have been the basic point for the whole system. The other two centers, Delphi and Sardis, are located on both sides of the meridian at an equal distance from it. Within a circle centered in Ammonium, they define an area 30 degrees wide, corresponding to one sign of the zodiac; the twelve signs cover 360°. Furthermore, the author notes that Delphi and Sardis are located on the same parallel. There is no doubt in his mind that this system of coordinates extended westward to the western Mediterranean. In his hypothesis, Malta and the city of Cumae in Italy function as the centers of reference for that region, as Delphi or Delos do for Greece.

The author's hypothesis is supported by the uniform decorative designs we find on many objects from the Orient, Egypt, and Greece: lions, griffins, rams, bulls, sirens, etc., all having an astrological reference. Certain symbols have always been associated with some constellations. Generally, animal forms are used, either real animals like the lion or the bull, or mythical ones such as griffins, centaurs, and sirens. As a result, the choice of a decorative design on a vase reveals its place of origin to the knowledgeable observer.

We might point out, however, that allusions to the astrological signs abound in Greek legend; yet their true meaning has been hidden until now. Perhaps Jean Richer's hypothesis is a beginning toward understanding them.

Reading his book prompts me to try to define the sites of the main Greek episodes in the *Odyssey* in relation to Delphi, which was the zodiacal center for that region:

Ulysses stays at Corfu and Ithaca; Telemachus, at Ithaca, Pylos, and Sparta. I draw a straight line joining each of these cities to Delphi. To my surprise, I discover that these lines retrace the zodiacal sections. From Corfu to Ithaca, Ulysses covers in one night an area of exactly 30 degrees; from Ithaca to Pylos, Telemachus covers two areas, or 60 degrees. From Pylos to Sparta, he covers still another area of 30 degrees. (See map No. 2.)

Finally, on his return trip to Sparta, Telemachus is at the western end of Elis at sunset. He again has cleared a 30-degree sector in relation to Delphi.

One more point: Pylos and Delos are on the same parallel. Is that a coincidence? Or did the writer choose these stages of the trip rather than others in order to suggest the system he is using for measuring directions, that is, a system based on 12 general bearings, each covering a 30-degree angle? The question is a hard one to answer, and I refrain from making a hasty decision. Yet I would not be surprised if Telemachus's trip to Sparta supplied once more, as it did for defining the ships' speed, a unit of measure, this time for defining bearings from a basic point of reference. Could it be, then, that the mythological events studding Ulysses' voyage, which I have deliberately ignored so far, and the allusion to animals so typical of the language of astrology have a precise geographical meaning?

Taking off from this new hypothesis, I re-examine every stage of Ulysses' trip to pick out the scenes possibly related to zodiacal signs or mentioning animals that represent a zodiacal sign or axis. Because of my limited acquaintance with such matters, I must depend on Jean Richer's comparative charts.

After 9 stormy days, Ulysses reaches a continent, the land of the Lotus-eaters. I had located this country in the south of Morocco, almost at the level of the Canaries, at about latitude 29° north. I notice immediately that this latitude is that of the oasis of Siwa, ancient Ammonium, which Jean Richer defines as the base of the Mediterranean system of coordinates. The allusion to the lotus, or Egyptian *nenuphar*, may mean that the right course will take the sailor along the African coast down to the latitude of Egypt's major sanctuary, the base point of the system of geographical coordinates used at the time.

Let us continue to the Cyclôpes' country. Ulysses and his companions owe their escape from the den of Polyphemus to rams. This allusion to the ram means, perhaps, that the land of the Cyclôpes is located in the direction of the Ram, or west, in relation to the previous place. In fact, that is geographically correct if we identify the Cyclôpes' archipelago as the Canary Islands. Ulysses returns to the island of Fuerteventura and from there sails toward Aeolia, or the island of the winds.

In astrological language, wind and air compare with Aquarius, symbol of air. It is surprising, then, to discover that the bearing for Madeira is exactly the one suggested by Aquarius, that is, northwest, forming a 30-degree angle with north.

After Madeira, Ulysses sails north, give or take a few degrees, and reaches the land of the giant Laestrygonians. There he meets the daughter of the king as she draws water from "the spring of the she-bear." According to Jean Richer, allusions to giants and to the Great Bear indicate a northerly direction, which is again in accord with my itinerary. The next stage is the island of Aea, Circe's home. The sorceress Circe is surrounded by wild animals, lions, wolves, etc., which she holds under a spell. Circe is evidently identified here with the goddess Artemis, mistress of wildlife. Furthermore, Artemis was traditionally accompanied by a hind. Now, the first animal Ulysses meets on the island is a deer. Jean Richer, in his explanation of the legend of the river Alpheus's pursuit of Artemis, submits that the story is an allusion to the axis Gemini-Sagittarius (southwest-northeast) forming a 30-degree angle with north. Homer himself gives an excellent confirmation of this theory in the *Odyssey*, Chapter XV, line 478, "Artemis the archer . . ."

So we have another surprising discovery: from the western tip of Ireland at the 54th parallel, around Achill island, the Laestrygonians' country, a 30° bearing east of north leads to the island of Barra, home of Circe. That is exactly the bearing of Sagittarius on the zodiacal wheel.

Pushed by Boreas, Ulysses sails due south toward Northern Ireland and the Cimmerians' country; there he calls on the dead in the dark home of Hades and Persephone, guardians of the infernal regions. In Greek mythology, the descent to those regions was traditionally placed at Cape Tenare, the southern tip of the Peloponnesus peninsula. The cape is located exactly on Delphi's meridian due south from Delphi.

After his return to Circe, Ulysses sails southeast toward the island of the Sirens.

According to Jean Richer, the Sirens, which at that time were always represented by birds, suggest the Aquarius-Leo line, a northwest-southeast direction, forming a 30-degree angle with the north-south axis. Once more, we can easily verify on the map that Ulysses must follow that direction from the island of Barra to reach the rocks of Charybdis and Scylla.

The next mythical character we meet is none other than Scylla, the hideous six-headed monster who strangely recalls the Hydra of Lerna who defeated Heracles in the marshes of Argolis in Greece. As it happens, "Hydra" is both a Greek island and a constellation near Leo that indicates a southeast direction forming a 30-degree angle with the south. The island of Hydra in Greece and Argolis where Lerna is situated are located in that very direction with relation to Delphi.

The island of Staffa with its murmuring cave are also located exactly in the direction of the constellation Hydra near Leo on the zodiacal wheel, in relation to the island of Coll, which Ulysses had just left.

Passing in front of Staffa, the ship can only be heading for the island of Mull. On that island (Thrinacia) graze the immortal cattle and sheep of Helios.

The Greek island of Seriphos, consecrated to Helios, is located southeast of Delphi. Mull, too, partly encircles Staffa on the southeast side; but there the meaning is less evident, especially since the allusion to cattle would make one think of the constellation Taurus, which signifies southwest. Certain code figures may thus have a meaning I cannot read for the moment. For example, on Thrinacia there are 7 herds of 50 cattle and as many sheep, that is, 700 animals. Likewise, when Ulysses arrives at the first island of the Cyclôpes' archipelago, 118 goats are killed to feed Ulysses and his men. Perhaps these figures stand for dates on an unknown calendar?

After the slaughter of the cattle, their remains miraculously shake themselves and begin to walk, probably to leave no doubt about their immortal nature. I learn from other sources that at that period, the end of the bronze age, ingots of precious metal were often moulded in the shape of oxen hides. This fact was proved by archeological findings from the Bronze Age.

Metal as matter could have been considered immortal, even though the blacksmiths gave it different shapes. There was also a rather widespread belief that linked metals to the sun's rays. Finally, the symbol of the ox was used on the first coins; even the name for the ancient coin *aes* derives from "ox."

In symbolic language, understood only by the initiated, these oxen hides may have meant ingots of precious metal. If that is the case, the slaughter of the immortal cattle on Thrinacia, which seems the object of the trip, could be translated as plunder of the precious metal by Ulysses' companions.

Farther on, we shall attempt to find the meaning of the maritime route described in light of modern archeological findings concerning the end of the Bronze Age. For now, we state only that a knowledge-

Ancient map of the sky employing mythological figures associated with stars and constellations.   *Photo: Giraudon*

able audience could understand the route with relative ease if we suppose that bearings were indicated by zodiacal allusions and by references to the winds.

The distance to be covered in a specific direction is expressed in terms of days of sailing when the trip is longer than 24 hours. The measure of distance for a single day derives from Telemachus's trips in Greece since there we deal with known distances. But how do we account for the shipwreck on the return trip as Ulysses leaves the island of Thrinacia? One can easily interpret that as an omen forbidding to the direction followed by Ulysses. To this day we post a skull and crossbones at a dangerous passage.

Teiresianiades the prophet, who had suggested the route for Ulysses to follow, specified that he sail past Thrinacia without doing harm to Helios' cattle. I would interpret this as a warning that this maritime route is suited only to a ship with no cargo and therefore fully maneuverable.

Unfortunately, Ulysses' companions did not resist the temptation, and Zeus's punishment fell on the ship.

All of this could mean, then, that a loaded ship must not follow Ulysses' course after leaving Thrinacia. What was this fateful bearing? The answer is simple: southwest. In fact, Ulysses refuses to leave Thrinacia so long as the winds are blowing south and east and would push him in the right direction, northwest. He leaves the island when the winds change. Then the west wind rises, the ship founders, and the wreckage is pushed by the south wind through the whole night, reaching Charybdis and Scylla at dawn.

The shipwreck site is located slightly southwest of Charybdis and Scylla. The fateful course must then be in the opposite direction. Now, in astrological language and in the zodiacal system of reference used to indicate directions, a direction is represented by a zodiacal axis, north-south for example, and the "opposite" direction—perpendicular to the preceding—would be west-east.

The direction to follow, consequently, is indicated by the sign opposed to the northeast-southwest axis, or the northwest-southeast diagonal, perpendicular to the former. Since Notus, the south wind, is pushing the ship's wreckage, it can only go northwest, in the direction of Iceland. At any rate, the exact course is given by the 9 days adrift in Ulysses' imaginary trip around Crete. The death of the pilot during the shipwreck warns us that we ought to change guides after that point. For, in that age, it was the pilot who figured the route according to the position of the stars.

The new guide must be once more the account of the drifting (transferred to Greece), which reveals both course and distance to the alert reader. The meaning then becomes clear: The homeward-bound ship, loaded with the carcasses of Helios's cattle, is struck by lightning as it attempts to retrace its original course by turning southwest.

The loaded ship, helped by the south wind, must pass Charybdis and Scylla again, which is geographically correct.

At Ogygia, or Iceland, some of the details about Calypso's cave are again possibly borrowed from astrological language. The vine on the cavern wall may allude to Dionysus who often appears on vases and shields along with other astrological signs. Most often his place is next to Aquarius. On the zodiacal wheel, that corresponds to a northwest direction, that of Iceland as one sets out from Scotland. The homeward route from Iceland, as we have pointed out earlier, is indicated by the position of the Great Bear and the constellation Pleiades in relation to the ship's progress. Calculation shows that Ulysses is heading south, an easy route for a sailboat. In summer the high-pressure areas are centered on Iceland. The prevailing winds, which in the Northern Hemisphere turn counterclockwise, blow south as they leave the high-pressure zone. Then, at lower latitudes they tend to change in an easterly direction.

Ulysses' round trip in the Atlantic is shaped like a long loop, elongated in the north-south direction. He covers it counterclockwise, heading north at the beginning of summer and returning south in the fall.

The return to Greece in a west-east direction from a point located off Gibraltar presents no particular problems, thanks to the prevailing west winds that propel the ship eastward at that season. When the text speaks of Ulysses' first attempt to return to Ithaca (from Aeolia), it implies that seasonal winds had pushed Ulysses' ship east for 9 days and nights.

Finally, the arrival at the island of Scheria provides another opportunity to verify the astral code. The first person whom Ulysses meets on arrival at Corfu is Nausicaa. She and her companions had come to do their laundry on the banks of a river. In Chapter VI, line 100 and following, Ulysses states:

When they had eaten enough, both maids and mistress, they threw off their veils and played ball, and Nausicaa led the singing,

with her white arms flashing in the sunlight as she threw the ball.
She looked like Artemis when, bow in hand, she comes down
from the mountains over lofty Taigetos or Erymanthos . . .

There is here a very clear identification between Nausicaa and
Artemis the Archer. We saw that the direction indicated by Sagittarius was the southwest-northeast diagonal, forming a 30-degree angle
with the north. That is the precise direction Ulysses followed to
Corfu after turning around the southern point of Sicily. Now an
important question arises: From the strict navigational point of view,
is our itinerary a logical one for a sailing ship to follow from the
Mediterranean to Scotland and back? Much depends on the answer
to this question. If the answer is affirmative, Ulysses' trip could well
be the description of a maritime route already known to certain ships
of that time, that is, in the twelfth century B.C. When Ulysses calls
Lamos, the Laestrygonians' city, "famous," he seems to imply that
all sailors know about the port. If, on the contrary, ours is not a
coherent and logical trip for a sailing ship, then one must consider
the trips as exceptional, and the meaning of the *Odyssey* would then
be different. In this debate, the proposed itinerary for reaching
Ireland and the Scottish islands seems to hold the advantage of
letting Ulysses benefit from the Canary current upon emerging from
the Strait of Gibraltar. Then, island-hopping up to Madeira, he pene-
trates far enough in to the Atlantic to head north, avoiding the risk
of being thrown on the Iberian coast by the prevailing west winds.
On the other hand, what could be the purpose of the detour by way
of Iceland on the homeward trip?

Certainly, the harder the ship is to handle, the more the navigator
must take into account the winds and the currents. At that period,
sailors must have preferred a long detour, even if that meant more
rowing, in order to reach a point where favorable winds would almost
certainly push the ship toward its final destination.

If it is true that this type of ship, sailing normally by a tail wind,
could at the most sail in a direction perpendicular to the wind's
direction but never beyond that, one can easily imagine that when
the Atlantic winds blow steadily from the west, the Bay of Biscay

could represent a real trap on the return from the British Isles. These ships find it very difficult, then, to round the northwestern corner of the Iberian Peninsula (the present Galicia) before sailing north-south along the Portuguese coast. On the other hand, a southerly course from Iceland to the proper latitude for an eastward turn does not seem to present this kind of problem. I leave the debate open.

V. IN SEARCH OF CIRCE AND SCYLLA

My plane has just taken off from Carthage, Tunisia. The hill of Byrsa overlooking the Gulf of Tunis and the two semicircular Punic ports leading to the sea by a narrow inlet grow smaller and smaller before my eyes. According to legend, Dido founded Carthage at the foot of that hill more than 8 centuries before Christ, after she fled from Tyre in Phoenicia. Several centuries later, the hill had acquired 700,000 inhabitants and became the great marketplace of the western Mediterranean, a way station and crossroads between the Atlantic and the Greek world. Conquered and leveled by the Romans, the metropolis was eventually rebuilt, but not much has remained of its former splendor. The villas and the gardens, built in tiers on the slopes, today lie in ruins.

The Swissair *Coronado* flies over the endless beach of Raouad, then veers north, leaving on our left the ruins of Utica engulfed in the alluvium from the Medjerda River. The Roman road, which leaves northward from the city, follows the ancient, now sand-covered ports and leads to the Roman bridge. Only the bridge's useless piers remain standing in a swamp; no river flows here now. The coastline on the left seems farther and farther away, while lakes Bizerte and Ichkeul still sparkle in the late-afternoon sunshine. Now the sea is below us, dark blue, sprinkled with white crests. We will soon reach the southern coast of Sardinia. I know that here, between Tunisia and Sardinia, I am crossing Ulysses' path for the first time.

Ulysses sailed over this sea three times, counting both directions on his outward voyage, and once on the return trip in a west-east course that took him to the island of Scheria (Corfu). I picture, for a moment, his fleet of twelve long, black, narrow ships heading west, pushed by a strong wind that inflates their square sails. There are about fifty men aboard each ship. At the moment, there is no need for rowing. The pilots, experienced in astronomy, familiar with the maritime routes and with the currents and winds, stand in the bows. Aft, another man holds the helm, a long oar kept at an angle on one side of the ship. They have just skirted the familiar shores of Sicily. By sailing night and day, they expect to clear in four days Hercules' columns, which their ancestors had explored several centuries before. The magnificient fleet carries with it great expectations; it is the symbol of the spirit of these sailors and merchants from the islands off the west coast of Greece: Ithaca, Zákinthos, Cephalonia, etc.

The *Coronado* now flies over Sardinia where archeological discoveries from Cretan and Mycenaean times show that commerce with Greece had existed several centuries before the Trojan War. To find Ulysses and his companions again, I do not have to make the long detours they were forced to make because of currents and winds. I prefer to head north and follow Hermes, who also used an aerial route. That "line" of Hermes represents a southeast-northwest radius from Olympus. After the scarlet coves of the Island of Beauty and the luminous whiteness of the Alps, the stopover at Geneva puts me back on Hermes' path. The British European Airlines' *Trident* now carries me northwest in the night. Paris sparkles below, then London's immense expanse with its vague limits, checkered by a network of orange or pale-yellow lights. A few days later, the London-Glasgow flight takes me to Scotland. I have chosen the most characteristic points of Ulysses' itinerary to verify my theory on the spot. I especially want to find the famous sites of Charybdis and Scylla that he so carefully describes. According to my calculations, it is here, in Scotland and in Northern Ireland, that the principal episodes of Ulysses' trip are located: the fateful meeting with the Laestrygonians, the wintering on Circe's island, the north-south round trip to the Cimmerians' land, the passage by the island of the Sirens, and right afterward, the whirlpool of Charybdis and Scylla's cave, and finally the island of Thrinacia, or Trident.

Glasgow will be our takeoff point for exploring the region. The airline pilot tells us that Glasgow is "an angel with a black face." The black façades of the nineteenth-century buildings *do* give a sinister impression, for they show the results of the first industrial boom that brought more than a million people to the city within a few decades. However, the gloom is soon dispelled by the traditional Scottish hospitality. Our first destination is the island of Barra, the site of Ulysses' sojourn with Circe according to our reckoning. The island belongs to the archipelago of the Outer Hebrides, that is, the islands forming the outer bulwark northwest of the Scottish coast. One hour and ten minutes flying time should bring me over the supposed site of Charybdis and Scylla. The plane awaiting us is a four-engine propeller-driven "Heron." It can carry fourteen passengers, seven on each side of a central aisle. The low altitude of the flight (6,000 feet or about 2,000 meters) and the wide portholes allow an excellent

Barra, island of the enchantress Circe. From this point Ulysses perceived the sea forming the "crown" and discovered the manor of Circe nestled in the vale near an oak grove.   *Photo: author*

view of the top of the cloud ceiling a few hundred meters below. Over the sea, the sky is clearer; the islands and beaches begin to appear. I watch for the island of Staffa and its famous cave, the geographical coordinates of which agree well with my calculations. I can clearly spot the island and the giant cave, but the whirlpool of Charybdis is simply nowhere, and the sea is very calm all around. I make up my mind just the same to investigate later on the spot. Right now I am watching a line of small islands that we fly over immediately after Staffa. They are the Treshnish islands, conveniently located on a south-east axis in relation to Barra, which makes them good prospects for the site of the famous rocks. Their low elevation, however, and their pleasant appearance do not seem to correspond to Homer's description. I feel rather disappointed, and my assurance wavers. However, the converging evidence still points undisputably to this area. I will take up that search again on the return trip. Let us first look at Barra. The island draws near; the hills are high enough but with gentle and regular slopes. White beaches, dark rocky promontories, and pastures dotted with white sheep decorate the landscape. The low-flying plane now heads toward the northern tip of the island, stirring up a flock of sea birds and wild rabbits whose burrows puncture the hill like a sponge. Judging by the map of the island and by the joking between the pilot and his passengers, who all seem to know one another, there is no landing strip. Passing first over a plank lean-to proudly bearing the sign "Airport," we are guided by a boy's arm signals to our eventual landing—on a beach bedecked with pools of sea water. The millions of seashells embedded in the sand make for a good, firm runway. We are obviously the only tourists among the passengers, and the pilot very naturally offers to circle over the island when we are ready to leave.

A taxi is waiting for us; it takes us by the only road, a circular one, to the southern coast at Castlebay where we find private lodging, for the only hotel has recently burned down. A castle on a rock in the center of the bay provides the indispensable romantic touch. The island once belonged to the MacNeil clan, formidable sixteenth-century pirates. A descendant of the MacNeils, an American architect, still lives in the castle during the summer months. The island is about ten kilometers in diameter. The highest point, in the southern part of the island, is 1,260 feet high, or a little over 400 meters. We make slow progress climbing through the heather under a blue sky and intense sun. From the peak we have a panoramic view of the sea from all sides of the island. Toward the south where Ulysses came from, the port of Castlebay does appear very well sheltered by the islands around it. Ulysses says: "We brought our ship to the shore in silence, into a harbor where ships could lie." He adds later: "I climbed to a high place where I had a look around. We are on an island which the sea encircles like a crown. The island is flat, and I saw smoke rising in the air above a coppice of bushes and trees." The island must have appeared flat to Ulysses, although he does speak of a rocky peak and of a valley, which indicate some elevation. (See map No. 8.)

From the summit one can clearly make out a small pine and sycamore grove at the end of a valley facing southeast. Although there are no longer oaks on the island, they are still found in abundance all along Scotland's western coast. For three thousand years the Hebrides have been progressively cleared of trees to provide grazing lands, or timber for shipbuilding, and fuel. Ulysses found the island wooded. At present there remain three small groves of a few dozen trees, including the one I can spot in the valley of Circe (pronounced "Kirke"). It is interesting to note that *kirk* is a very common syllable in Gaelic, an ancient Celtic language still in current use in the Hebrides and in some parts of the Scottish mainland. The most important town of the Shetlands, which lie north of Scotland, is Kirkwall. This radical *kirk* is commonly found in the names of places in Ireland and Britain. It is believed that the Gaels, the oldest Celtic tribe, probably invaded the British isles about 1300 B.C. That would be more than a century before the fall of Troy, the opening event of the *Odyssey*. Hence, Kirk could be the name of a local goddess whom the Achaeans identified with Artemis, the mistress of wild animals usually pictured with a deer.

We begin our descent on the southeast side toward an elevated stone. Specimens found on the island of Barra indicate that the place was populated before 2000 B.C. The inhabitants, contemporaries of the Achaeans, left other traces of their activity at two locations along

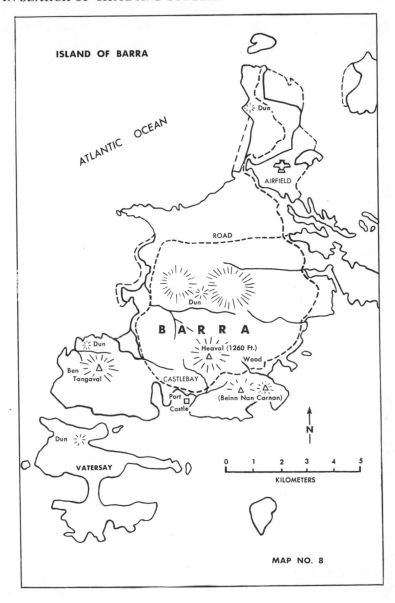

ISLAND OF BARRA

ATLANTIC OCEAN

Dun

AIRFIELD

ROAD

Dun

B A R R A

Dun

Ben
Tangaval

Heaval (1260 Ft.)

Wood

CASTLEBAY

Port
Castle

(Beinn Nan Carnan)

N

Dun

VATERSAY

0   1   2   3   4   5

KILOMETERS

MAP NO. 8

the western coast of the island, one in the southern part and the other at the northern tip where a long, white, sandy beach ends. Walking along this coast in the evening before sunset, I found the remains of two prehistoric forts built on promontories with a commanding view of the entire western coast facing the Atlantic. They are circular structures made of roughly hewn blocks stacked dry without cement or mortar. Traces of fire intense enough to have melted sand or stone into glass have been found there. Did the structures serve as ancient foundries? The location of those forts on headlands near the sea would rather indicate to me an activity related to seafaring. Perhaps they were beacons burning wood for light?

It is hard to imagine on these islands at the end of the world and at an age so removed in time a seafaring activity so intensive that it would have made such installations necessary. One fact is certain, however: the elevated stones, several dolmens, and the circular structures typical of solar cults prove that the island was populated at the time that concerns us. Furthermore, the density of that population implies economic activities capable of feeding the people of the island.

At about 10:15 P.M., local time, the sun sets over the sea, the outlines of the prehistoric fort fade away, and we walk back in the long twilight across the wild fields of briar, past granite slabs rounded and streaked by glacial erosion. This kind of landscape is typical of the Alps at altitudes above 1,000 meters; here we find it at sea level. I remember the passage from the *Odyssey* in which Ulysses, describing his arrival at Charybdis and Scylla, states that the rock is so smooth that it appears "polished." The term could well apply to these slabs, polished by the glaciers. The only areas in Europe where rocks are so polished by glaciers along the coast are in Scandinavia and Scotland. This observation assures me that I am on the right track. Now I am full of hope for the second stage of our search, that of Charybdis and Scylla.

Next day, we head for the promontory that marks the southeastern corner of the island. I am hypothetically and secretly hoping against all sane hope to find a trace of the site of Elphenor's grave; he was the drunken sailor whom Ulysses had cremated, then buried under a large stone "on the highest ground of the foreland." The stone must have been engraved to mark the site. I chose the promontory called "Beinn nan Charnan" because it faces southeast toward Greece. I think that the leader of a faraway expedition would want to place such a grave on a peak; that way, later visitors to the island could verify that he had been there. That would explain the phrase "on the summit" in the *Odyssey*. I also think that he would prefer a slope facing his native land. We climb up rolling slopes covered with briars, spotted here and there by lamb carcasses picked at by the birds.

From the peak, I glance at the endless sea toward Greece, then start down a few meters in that direction. The peak is the top of a tall vertical rock wall slanted toward the sea. In the middle of this wall, I notice an obviously rectangular depression that is several meters long. On the inner side, the surface of the rock shows a series of cracks, sometimes rectilinear, vertical or horizontal, sometimes rounded. Is this a work of nature? Or is it an ancient inscription whose author wished to protect it from erosion by digging deeper into the vertical wall, thus creating a protective frame? The idea seems far-fetched, and I am reluctant to commit myself. I do find, though, a mound consisting of large rocks piled against the wall where it meets the southeastern slope. I cannot help thinking that it is perhaps there one will find the urn with Elphenor's ashes. I leave the spot reluctantly since I would like to spend more time there. Back with our pleasant hostess at Castlebay, I review in my mind the results of the exploration of Barra before I board our *Heron* at the airport on the north beach. I am not disappointed, for I have found that most of the conditions are met for considering Barra as Circe's island. It is situated right along the route Ulysses would have followed from the last stopover in western Ireland. At a day's journey to the south, we find land and a river with a deep mouth. The island's size is still another indication: It is neither so large that one could not see from the peak the sea forming a crown about it, nor is it so small that its resources would not have allowed the local population and their guests to pass the winter comfortably. The oak groves producing acorns for feeding swine also add to the probability.

The *Heron* is late; some technical trouble has prevented it from taking off on schedule, so we are told by the officer in charge in his wooden cabin at the airport as he keeps an eye on the kettle for the pilot's tea. The cabin serves both as a checkroom for luggage and as a control tower for the plane's landing. To while away the time, he suggests we have tea in a comfortable farmhouse near the beach, our runway. We are glad to comply, for now the sky is low and it is raining. Three hours later, the *Heron* drops out of the clouds and lands on the sand with a great splashing of water puddles. After taking off, the plane slowly climbs over the sea, leaving behind the island's highest peak, its long white beaches, its headlands, and its coves. An hour later, we drop into a valley between the hilltops that is sprinkled with white sheep; then the *Heron* lands at Glasgow. The first stage of my scouting is over; the most important stage is about to begin.

A day in Glasgow gives me the opportunity to stroll through the alleys bordering Buchanan Street. In a specialized bookstore, I buy some topographical maps and a well-documented book on the Hebrides and the sea around them. (See map No. 9.)

We take off again, this time by land northward along Loch Lomond, which is wedged between the mountains. Under a cloudy sky the Scottish bus surmounts some desolate mountain passes and eventually lets us off at the small port of Oban on the western coast of the Highlands.

My intention is to get as near as possible to the presumed site of Charybdis and Scylla. A calculation of their distance from Iceland has given me their coordinates. Nine days of drifting from this point led Ulysses to Iceland. The story of the fictitious drift in the Mediterranean from southern Crete to the land of the Thesprotians had allowed me to calculate a certain number of degrees covered in latitude and longitude starting from the coordinates of a point on the western coast of Iceland. My deduction led me to a site very close to Staffa, famous for Fingal's Cave. If that was indeed Scylla's den, I should be able to find two islands of unequal elevation in the vicinity and, near the cave, Charybdis's whirlpool, which comes alive three times during the day.

On leaving Oban, our ship enters the Sound of Mull, a long strait separating the island of Mull from the Scottish mainland. On our left at the end of the island of Kerrera, we pass a herd of seals tumbling about on the rocks and looking at us congenially. We stop at Tobermory, then head south in order to circle Mull and approach the Treshnish. This series of small islands is within the scope of my research for two reasons. First, their coordinates fit my previous calculations. Second, they are located, like Staffa, on a line beginning at Barra on a northwest-southeast axis forming a 30-degree angle to the north-south diagonal. I had come upon this by analyzing the episode of the Sirens, those mythical birds representing the constellation Aquarius. Unfortunately, as my aerial view several days before had led me to suspect, the islands' appearance does not match Homer's text. Their elevation is too low, and there is no strait between them that would qualify as the only passage. Their basaltic

The island of Staffa, where the preliminary hypothesis had situated Scylla's cave. However, the whirlpool of Charybdis was not properly located in relation to it.

Photo: author

structure is clearly favorable to cave formation, but the sea around us is perfectly calm, and a whirlpool is nowhere in sight. I shift my hopes to Staffa, which we are now approaching. Here, the view is definitely striking. The caves—for the island has several—are monumental. Their walls are basalt columns, crystallized in hexagonal sections. They truly resemble cathedral vaults. It is easy to imagine here the den of some terrible monster. But once more, Charybdis's whirlpool is missing. There is no use pretending any longer that Staffa is Scylla's den or waiting for the whirlpool to appear at the foot of the rock.

I am bitterly disappointed; however, the pleasant and interesting stop at the sacred island of Iona comes in time to comfort me. The island—green, sunny, and encircled by white, sandy beaches—emerges from a very blue transparent sea. The houses are low and built of dark granite with flower-bedecked windows. St. Columba came here in 563 A.D. to evangelize the Picts, the inhabitants of the Hebrides. The island became a shrine, and one can visit the flowery ruins of a thirteenth-century Romanesque church. Farther on, near another church that has been restored, an ancient paved road leads to a magnificent eleventh-century Celtic cross. Tall weeds a few feet from there hide the carved granite figures of several Scottish kings of the high Middle Ages.

It has often been noted that shrines keep their religious function even when new arrivals spread a different faith. We know for a fact that in many Celtic areas Christian shrines have sprung up at sites formerly dedicated to Druid cult.

The monks who evangelized the people were thus more sure of eliminating all traces of the former cult and changing the ancient pagan festivities into holy days of the new religion. Thanks to its favorable location off Mull, Iona must have always been a center of meetings and trade. Lighter ships sailing north-south along the Scottish coast could not help but stop there. The ancient Gaelic name for the island was *Innis nan Druinish*, or Island of the Druids. Iona must have been an important Celtic site in pre-Christian times. There are also on this island prehistoric traces of circular buildings, proof that the area was settled in a very early age. As we leave Iona,

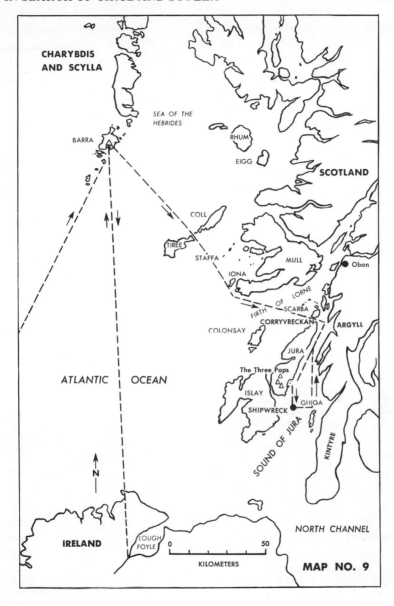

CHARYBDIS
AND SCYLLA

SEA OF THE
HEBRIDES

BARRA

RHUM

EIGG

SCOTLAND

COLL

TIREE

STAFFA

IONA

MULL

Oban

FIRTH OF LORNE

SCARBA

CORRYVRECKAN

COLONSAY

ARGYLL

JURA

The Three Paps

ATLANTIC   OCEAN

ISLAY

GIIIGA

SHIPWRECK

SOUND OF JURA

KINTYRE

N

IRELAND

LOUGH
FOYLE

NORTH CHANNEL

0   50

KILOMETERS

MAP NO. 9

I notice that we are heading on a line that very nearly corresponds to that northwest-southeast route suggested by Circe at the departure from Barra. I must be, then, on the right road; but the few skimpy islands on my right and the cliffs of Mull on my left show nothing resembling either the famous strait or Charybdis' whirlpool.

Tired of scanning the horizon, I lower my disappointed gaze to my companions who, sheltered from the north wind. are warming themselves on the bridge. It is then that I *see the whirlpool*—in an illustrated booklet one of the passengers next to me is leafing through. I buy the brochure for a few shillings and learn that there is a famous whirlpool called the "Whirlpool of Corryvreckan" in a strait between two islands several miles south of our present site. The information is exciting enough to make me spend that evening and part of the night inspecting maps and documents, especially W. H. Murray's book on the Hebrides. He has an entire chapter devoted to

Above, the cave of Cailleach on the island of Scarba.   *Photo: author*

Right, the whirlpool with slopes of the island of Scarba rising sharply above it.
                                                                    Photo: Jack House

that famous spot. What I learn strikes me as extremely interesting. There is a large channel here whose general orientation is north-south or, more precisely, north-northeast-south-southwest, bounded on the west by Islay and Jura islands. The latter separate the channel from the open sea. On the east, the channel is bounded by the Kintyre peninsula and the coast of Argyll County. This channel becomes narrower toward the north where the surging of the rising and descending tide causes violent coastal currents. At this spot, the channel joins the open sea through a strait located between the northern tip of Jura and the small island of Scarba. It is in the passage between the two islands, when the ebb and flow are strongest, that a whirlpool occurs.

When this phenomenon is reinforced by a strong surge from the Atlantic, the noise of the surf can be heard for several miles around. Light-tonnage ships, unless they clear the strait when the sea is slack, risk being sucked in and may break up on the rocks. According to W. H. Murray, the strait's legendary reputation is justified. Apart from his personal experience while pleasure-boating in the passage in 1959, he quotes several examples of ships in trouble in this strait.

According to ancient Scottish legends, the strait is haunted by a sorceress named Cailleach who causes ships to founder. She is said to live in a cave located exactly above the whirlpool. Such a cave, of large dimensions, does exist there. Murray recommends, somewhat roguishly, I think, that his readers camp at the cave to observe better the whirlpool and to absorb the dramatic and legendary atmosphere of the forbidding spot. I cannot help immediately linking the Gaelic legend to the Scylla episode. The Gaelic sorceress's name, Cailleach, resembles that of Scylla's mother, Crataïs. Circe uses that name when Ulysses suggests defending himself with his sword against Scylla: "Scylla is not mortal; she is rather an immortal scourge . . . Instead, pass her quickly; call on Scylla's mother, Crataïs, to help you. It is she who bore this scourge of men . . ." How many coincidences!

The present name of the strait, "Corryvreckan," is derived from ancient Gaelic and supposedly means "whirlpool of Breacan." The name appears for the first time in the glossary of Cornac, king of Munster and bishop of Cassel from 901 to 908. The story has it that

Breacan, king of Ireland, foundered at the strait with fifty ships. The disaster must have occurred much earlier, though, for Breacan is not a Celtic Christian name but an ancient Gaelic one. The ships were probably coracles, that is, ancient round boats made from hides on a wooden frame. The event also left traces in Irish legends that, however, locate it in the strait separating Northern Ireland from Rathlin Island. According to Nordic legends, Breacan was the son of the king of Norway. He was engulfed by the whirlpool under romantic circumstances. Wishing to do some daring deed for the love of a woman, he swore to spend three days in a boat in Corryvreckan's whirlpool. He had three anchor ropes especially woven. One was of wool, one of hemp, and one of the hair of a virgin. The first rope broke the first night; the second the next night; the virgin's hair yielded strand by strand until, at the last hour, the last strand broke. The boat, engulfed by the whirlpool, was carried under. Breacan's body, found later, was buried in a neighboring cave called *Uamh Brecain*, on the southern coast of the strait.

A great many legends refer to that spot and involve both the whirlpool that engulfs boats and the cave located nearby. The parallel between these old legends and the story of Charybdis and Scylla is especially striking. The comparison is not new, for Adamnan, St. Columba's sixteenth-century biographer, speaking of the dangers experienced by the saint's companions, mentions a "Charybdis Braecanis," a term rather similar to the present name Corryvreckan. In general, place names are stable; nations disappear, but the name remains. The invader preserves the sounds of the name while transposing it into his own language.

This time I am sure of being on the right track, and the negative results of my cruise to Staffa are forgotten. That evening, I have trouble going to sleep; I keep shuffling the new data in my mind, and I am anxious to verify them on the spot.

The next day I go down to the harbor to find out how to reach Corryvreckan's whirlpool. Luck has it that the MacBraynes Company is sending one of its ships to the strait the following day. The ship is to use the approach best suited for my purpose, that is, from the west.

After leaving Oban, the ship enters Loch Linnhe, which extends northeast, becoming narrower as the mountains bordering it become higher. The very narrow bed of Loch Linnhe ends at Fort William at the foot of Ben Nevis, Great Britain's highest peak with an altitude of 1,400 meters. We turn our back on that magnificent view in order to head southwest toward the Firth of Lorne. Leaving the southern coast of Mull on our right, we imperceptibly strike a southern direction. As we are approaching Scarba from the northwest, the island appears to have a high altitude, whereas in fact its highest elevation is only 500 meters. Toward the west and the south, the slopes are very steep. On the western side, a stream cascades from the upper plateau to the shore. The waterfall hides immense slabs of granite, smoothed and streaked by glacial erosion.

We are now facing the strait and eventually cross it in a west-east direction. On the left, the monumental pyramid of Scarba rises, with its steep and smooth slopes. The right shore, the northern part of the

The island of Jura, seen from Corrievreckan.   *Photo: author*

island of Jura, is much lower. It consists of a low plateau that drops sharply to become an arid bank sprinkled with caves behind small, pointed islands. In the middle of the strait the sea looks different. The ground waves break sharply and run counter to great circles of eddies whose center is completely smooth, as if the water were rising from the depths of the strait to fold under again around the periphery of the circle. Today the weather is fine; the sky is cloudless, and there is not a breath of wind. Under these conditions it is hard to realize the effect produced by the Atlantic waves breaking against those circular currents. At the center of some of those large, smooth circles, spiral-shaped whirlpools absorb the surface water as if some deep hole were sucking the sea water down.

On a calm sea the scene is definitely not too striking. But the still unusual appearance of the waters, the large circles bordered with foam, rising eddies, and spiral whirlpools, do convey an uneasy and anxious feeling. One can easily imagine the difference in the scene during rough weather when the tidal current is at its strongest. Sailors from that area claim that the noise of the surf can be heard for several miles around. From personal experience, W. H. Murray compares it to an artillery barrage. Ulysses says in Chapter XII, line 202: "Presently I saw smoke and a great wave, and heard the sea roaring." The strait is two miles long from east to west and one mile wide. According to nautical information, the tidal current reached nine knots. Sailing ships with light tonnage are strongly advised to keep clear of Corryvreckan's passage, for they risk being thrown upon the rocks. All of the many legends relating to Corryvreckan attribute a ship's survival or destruction to the mood of Cailleach, the female demon supposedly living in one of the caves overlooking the whirlpool. We ourselves clear the whirlpool; Cailleach, alias "Circe's Crataïs," is kind to us. I look for her den and find that from front starboard two vast caves appear at the foot of the southern wall of Scarba, that is, on the northern bank of the strait. The second, in an east-west direction, seemingly the larger, could be Cailleach's legendary den. Its entrance faces west. From the other side, on the southern bank of the strait, the topographical map shows numerous caves, hardly visible from the sea. Breacan, the unfortunate king shipwrecked at Corryvreckan, must be buried in one of them. A raised stone in the cave should mark the site. With great difficulty, W. H. Murray explored that especially wild northwestern coast of Jura. He thinks he found the cave, but there was no sign of a grave.

The whole coast is deserted and difficult to reach. No road crosses it; the land is untilled. The coast itself is very rocky and falls abruptly into the sea. It is directly exposed to the waves from the northwest. Let us see what the text says. Circe tells Ulysses of two routes that will be available to him: "On the one side there are beetling rocks, and against them the great wave roars of dark-eyed Amphitrite. These, ye must know, are they the blessed gods call the Rocks Wandering." That sentence seems to describe the entrance to the straits and the two rocky masses that border it on the north and south.

By this way even winged things may never pass, not even cowering doves that bear ambrosia to Father Zeus, but the sheer rock evermore takes away one even of these, and the Father sends in another to make up the tale.

To my mind, that sentence refers to the smooth rock of Scarba's slopes; the allusion to the dove and to Zeus probably means that the observer must look north for the rock toward the constellation of Columba. The latter is on the Gemini-Sagittarius axis, which forms toward the northeast a 30-degree angle with the north. That is Scarba's position.

. . . The other rock was never cleared by any ship with a human burden . . . Only one ship on a long voyage was able to clear it, the Argo, which all the poets compete in praising, on its return to the land of Aletes. If Hera had not let the ship pass, because of her friendship with Jason, the waves would have quickly cast the ship against the large rocks.

The allusion to the constellation of the Argonauts is clear; a sky chart shows that these stars are located in the same direction as Cancer. Knowing the connection between the signs of the zodiac and spatial bearings, we know that Cancer represents the south. The reference to Hera, Zeus's wife, only confirms the description of a north-south axis for the two rocks that border the strait. Let us continue reading the text point by point.

> On the other part are two rocks, whereof the one reaches with sharp peak to the wide heavens, a dark cloud encompasses it; this never streams away, and there is no clear air about the peak neither in the summer nor in harvest time. No mortal man may scale it or set foor thereon, not though he had twenty hands and feet. For the rock is smooth and sheer, as it were polished.

With some Mediterranean exaggeration, that description applies rather well to Scarba, with its pyramidal shape, and its slabs smoothed and planed down by glaciers.

> In the midst of the cliff is a dim cave turned to Erebus ... whereby ye shall even steer your hollow ship ... therein dwelleth Scylla, yelping terribly.

That cave, facing west, does in fact exist at the foot of Scarba's slopes, at the narrowest point of the strait. It is the one where Celtic tradition places Cailleach's den. Circe specifies: "That other cliff, Odysseus, thou shalt note, lying lower, hard by the first . . ." That is exact since the southern bank of the strait is much lower than Scarba Island.

". . . Beneath it mighty Charybdis sucks sown black water, for thrice a day she spouts it forth, and thrice a day she sucks it down in terrible wise." In fact, the three tides cover a period of about eighteen hours and twenty minutes, which corresponds to a day's length at that altitude during the "long days" of the June solstice. The two routes open to Ulysses, who is coming from the northwest, seem obvious. There is the southern route, which would take Ulysses along Jura's inhospitable northwestern coast. Circe is plainly against this choice, for only the Argonauts' ship was able to escape from its dangers. The other route lies between the two islands in the strait facing Scylla's cave toward the east, with a rock to the north and another to the south. To avoid Charybdis's whirlpool, Ulysses must head for the cave. It is an easy mark, since its opening, facing west appears as soon as he enters the strait.

Ulysses did precisely that. By following the northwest-southeast axis to which the Siren's episode referred, he arrives in view of the strait. Continuing on that line, he must see in front of him the northern coast of Jura. On Circe's advice, he will now head east to enter the strait. It is Ulysses who directs the maneuver.

> Soon as we left the isle, thereafter presently I saw smoke and a great wave, and heard the sea roaring ... "helmsman, thus I charge thee, and ponder it in thine heart, seeing that thou wieldest the helm of the hollow ship. Keep the ship well away from this smoke and from the wave and hug the rocks, lest the ship, ere thou art aware, start from her course to the other side, and so thou hurl us into ruin." So I spake, and quickly they hearkened to my words.

Ulysses is in fact heading for the cave, for he specifies later:

> I went on to the decking of the prow, for thence methought that Scylla of the rock would be first seen, who was to bring woe on my company. Yet could I not spy her anywhere, and my eyes waxed weary for gazing all about toward the darkness of the rock.
> Next we began to sail up the narrow strait lamenting. For on the one hand lay Scylla, and on the other mighty Charybdis in terrible wise sucked down the sea water. As often as she belched it forth, like a cauldron on a great fire ...

Ulysses probably avoids the middle of the strait where the whirlpools and the currents are strongest and goes along Scarba's coast near the caves.

Our own ship has now cleared the strait and entered the wide corridor between Jura and County Argyll.

Circe had said to Ulysses: "Then thou shalt come on to the isle Thrinacia; there are the many kine of Helios and his brave flocks feeding."

Thrinacia might be translated as "Trident." I think one can interpret the name as meaning an island with three teeth or points. Standing on starboard and looking southeast, I discover with surprise

three peaks that clearly stand out against the horizon. Their characteristic pyramidal shape makes them noticeable from far away. They
are actually located in the southern part of Scarba.

Today called The Three Paps, they reach an altitude of about 850
meters. The first, on the east, is Beinn [Shiantaidh,] which means
"Holy Mountain." The middle peak, the highest, is called ["Beinn an
Oir,"] often interpreted as "mountain of gold." The last and southernmost peak, [Beinn Chaolais,] overlooks the strait separating Jura
from Islay. These three mountains are of quartzite, a hard primitive
rock with a mixture of quartz and basalt. Knowing that auriferous
lodes often consist of auriferous quartz inserted in the cracks of the
granite, one would not find it surprising that the main peak is called
"Mountain of Gold."

Leaning against the rail, I can hardly remove my gaze from those
three "paps" that could so easily be called "three points" (Trident).
They appear as soon as we have cleared the strait. Ulysses' next
sentence shows that Thrinacia is very close to Charybdis and Scylla:

Now when we had escaped the Rocks and dread Charybdis and
Scylla, thereafter we soon came to the fair island of the god; where
were goodly kine, broad of brow, and the many brave flocks of
Helios Hyperion.

Since it was getting dark, Ulysses' men urged him to disembark.
However, Ulysses made them first swear not to touch the sacred
cattle:

Now after they had sworn and done the oath, we stayed our
well-builded ship in the hollow harbour near to a well of sweet
water . . .

We must sail a while southeast along the eastern coast of Jura to
find a port with steep banks. We find it at the southern part of the
island near the "three points" where there is a bay well protected
from the open sea by some small islands. I also note that Helios's
cattle on that island could be a reference to the constellation Taurus.
According to our code, that would indicate a southeast direction.
Once again, the zodiacal code proves reliable, for the three peaks are
indeed in a southeast direction. But, by a strange coincidence, that

eastern coast of Jura is also known for its fine meadows and herds of
cattle. Also in this spot, traces of human settlement go back to
prehistoric times. At the southern tip of the island, a *menhir* (Celtic:
long stone) more than four meters high overlooks the strait separating
Jura from Islay. Its erection probably dates back to 1600 B.C. four
centuries before Ulysses' voyage. The caves on the northwest coast,
mentioned in many legends, have for a long time served as shelter for
both sailors and cattle.

Ulysses' ship, then, is anchored in that bay on the eastern coast
of Jura. The coastline here is more or less straight, and the bank
forms a northeast-southwest line with the open sea to the southeast.
That geographical position agrees perfectly with the text that follows.
The storm is in progress and the ship is confined in the bay.

"Then for a whole month the South Wind blew without ceasing,
and no other wind arose, save only the East and the South." It is
clear that as long as the east and south winds blow the ship cannot
set sail, for those winds would push the ship north or west, against
the coast.

Again, there is sufficient agreement with the text. Ulysses' starved
companions break down and eventually butcher the sacred cattle.
Their misdeed draws Zeus's punishment on the ship. Once the storm
is over, they set sail and reach the open sea. "When we left that isle
nor any land appeared, but sky and sea only." The ship is struck by
lightning, Ulysses' companions drown, and Ulysses himself hangs on
to the ship's wreckage. At that moment, there was a west wind, for
we read:

> Then verily the West Wind ceased to blow with a rushing storm,
> and swiftly withal the South Wind came, bringing sorrow to my
> soul, that so I might again measure back that space of sea, the
> way to deadly Charybdis. All the night I was borne, but with the
> rising of the sun I came to the rock of Scylla, and to dread
> Charybdis.

This text shows clearly that the shipwreck site is located south-
southeast of the strait of Charybdis and Scylla. In fact, the wreckage
is first pushed a short while toward the east by Zephyr, then the
whole night by the south wind. I had already figured that the night's

drifting covered a little less than 50 kilometers. In Ulysses' fictional trip, the speed of the drift is about 100 kilometers for each twenty-four-hour period. Back in my hotel room at Oban's port that evening, I again searched the maps of the Hebrides to verify two important points.

The first concerns the stage Ulysses completed between leaving Circe and arriving at Thrinacia. Evidently, he had set sail at sunrise.

> So spake she, and anon came the golden-throned Dawn. Then the fair goddess took her way up the island. But I departed my ship and roused my men themselves to mount the vessel and loose the hawsers. And speedily they went aboard and sat upon the benches, and sitting orderly smote the gray sea water with their oars.

By Eurylochus's speech, we know that it is getting dark when they decide to put in at the island of Thrinacia. They must have been sailing all day long. When Ulysses finished his trip to the land of the Cimmerians (after the island of Aea), the wind had been filling his sails from sunrise to sunset. Hence, the suggested itinerary from Circe to Thrinacia must equal in sailing distance that covered by Ulysses on his preceding trip. If I am correct in identifying Charybdis with the Corryvreckan whirlpool, Barra must be just as far from the northern coast of Ireland as the distance Ulysses covered between Barra and the southeastern coast of Jura, passing by Corryvreckan. With relief, I see on the maps that in both cases the distance covered approximates 190 kilometers. I also notice that the distance amounts to nearly half of the full day's sailing previously used to determine the itinerary. I remember that a "full day" corresponds to about 380 kilometers, according to our key.

There was a second point I had to verify, the possibility of a shipwreck site at fifty kilometers south-southwest of the strait between the islands of Islay and Gigha. From this point, the wreckage could be pushed east to the northern tip of Gigha Island, then north the whole night. It is important to note that as long as the south wind is blowing, Ulysses knows he must return to Charybdis and Scylla. The orientation of this sea corridor, with Islay and Jura on one side and the Scottish coast on the other, given a strong south wind and the tidal current, would force a shipwrecked vessel to pass through the strait of Corryvreckan. In fact, this corridor, facing an obvious north-south, becomes narrower toward the north; its main exit to the open sea is the strait between Jura and Scarba.

"All the night I was borne, but with the rising of the sun I came to the rock of Scylla, and to dread Charybdis. Now she had sucked down her salt sea water . . . Steadfast I clung till she should spew forth mast and keel again." Ulysses takes advantage of this second trip to make a new observation. Hanging on to a tree, he lets the whirlpool engulf the wreckage, and waits for it to reappear. He marks the time of the ship's disappearance, daybreak. "Late they came to my desire. At the hour when a man rises up from the assembly and goes to supper, one who judges the many quarrels of the young men that seek him for law, at that same hour those timbers came forth to view from out Charybdis."

Court sessions in the ancient Greek marketplace must have started in the morning to end in time for the midday meal, before the afternoon heat. Hence, Ulysses sees the same water that swallowed his ship return before him at noon. But what time did the sun rise? Ulysses stayed a month on Thrinacia. He has been now sailing for three days. That yields a total of 33 or 34 days since the June solstice; he returns by Charybdis and Scylla around July 25. At that latitude, on that day, the sun rises about 3:40 A.M. The wreckage was invisible from 3:40 to noon, that is, for 8 hours and 20 minutes. Since it made a round trip out toward the sea and back, it was on its way out for 4 hours and 10 minutes. That is to say, the sea was slack 4 hours and 10 minutes after the disappearance of the wreckage, or at 7:50 A.M. One wonders what could be the purpose of this information, which obviously could be calculated more precisely. Did Ulysses use this method to indicate the year in which his expedition took place? By reconstructing the tidal tables of those early times about 1200 B.C., the supposed date of the fall of Troy, we could eventually determine in what year, on a July 25 and at latitude 56° north, the tide was either at its highest or lowest point about 8 A.M.

It would be quite exciting thus to stumble upon the date of the fall of Troy since we know that the major part of Ulysses' voyage takes place the year following the end of the war.

It would also be interesting to verify whether this procedure yields a date close to the current archeologically and historically figured dates for the Troyan War. If, indeed, the two dates coincide, one might imagine that Ulysses wished to transmit over thirty centuries, to his faraway descendants, the date of his trip. Be this as it may, we are presently concerned with an exact scientific observation about the hour of the tide.

I feel ready now to submit that all that part of the itinerary from Aea, Circe's land, to the faraway Ogygia of Calypso is established with precision. There is little doubt that Charybdis and Scylla correspond to the strait of Corryvreckan. Therefore, calculation of the length of Ulysses' trip—of leaving Circe at sunrise and arriving at Thrinacia at night—confirms that Barra is indeed the island of Aea.

One point still remains to be explained. Which island did Circe mean when she said that Ulysses must face the ordeal of the Sirens? That episode is plainly a mythological one and aims at indicating the direction to take. By the same token, the island must truly exist. Ulysses must, in succession, slip through between the islands of Tiree and Coll and then skirt Iona before reaching the strait between Scarba and Jura.

At least two islands are located at this part of the route, and I must admit that a fault appears here in my structure; nevertheless, I lean toward Iona. It seems always to have been an important religious site. The Druids were there before the arrival of Saint Columban and his disciples. Religious rites almost always incorporate liturgical hymns to please the faithful. The Sirens claim universal knowledge:

> None hath ever driven by this way in his black ship, till he hath heard from our lips the voice sweet as the honeycomb, and hath had joy thereof and gone on his way the wiser. For lo, we know all things . . . and we know all that shall hereafter be upon the fruitful earth.

One may imagine that the Siren's song, which claims to communicate wisdom, is a reference to the celebration of some very ancient religious cult. Perhaps that celebration implied an unlucky end for strangers, and for that reason Circe advised Ulysses not to stop at the island.

Since I know now the exact coordinates of Charybdis and Scylla, I can follow the itinerary in its normal direction and ascertain whether the nine days adrift really lead to Iceland.

Ulysses' description of the nine-day drift in the Mediterranean can also be figured with greater precision. I remember that the supposed Mediterranean shipwreck site is located at a latitude of 32.5° north and approximately on the meridian 26° east of Greenwich. This meridian cuts vertically across the eastern part of Crete and is the classical route of ships leaving Crete for Libya when they are coming from Phoenicia, that is, from the east. That is the route described by Ulysses.

The point of arrival is located in the land of the Thesprotians, or at the southern part of the present Albania. Luckily, it seems that the area has not changed its name for three thousand years. On a road map of Greece, compiled by Kuemmerly and Frey in Bern, we read: "Thesprotia, on the Western coast of Greece, opposite Corfu Island." The name has been preserved, but one wonders if the region coincides with that of Ulysses' time. It has been established for other regions of Greece that the name of a province followed the people's migration. In more remote times, people tended to migrate south. The original region, then, of Homer's Thesprotia was probably located slightly north of the present location that goes by the same name today. For that reason, I visited the northern end of Thesprotia at the spot where the coast is cut by the 40th parallel. There was another reason for choosing that spot. Ulysses spends one night with the Thesprotians; the next day one of their ships returns him to Ithaca by sunset. Hence, they sailed one full day. According to the average speed previously used for our calculations, the distance would be 190 kilometers north of Ithaca. I then notice a strange correspondence. The points of departure and arrival of the 9-day drifting are located, respectively, on the meridian of the city of Troy and on the parallel of the same city, thus forming with Troy a right-angled triangle. Troy is at the apex, along the 40th parallel north.

Furthermore, the triangle is of a very special kind. Proceeding north along the meridian that is the west side of the triangle, we find that the distance between the starting point of the drift and Troy is 7.5° of latitude. Taking this degree of latitude as a unit of measure, I discover that the small side of the triangle, between Troy and the arrival point on the 40th parallel, measures 5° of latitude, or 555 kilometers. The large side is, then, one and a half times the small side. The two acute angles of the triangle, the departure and arrival points, measure exactly 30 and 60 degrees. The drift's direction is perfectly defined: southeast-northwest, forming a 30-degree angle with the north. In zodiacal language, that is the exact direction expressed by the Leo-Aquarius axis. It is also perpendicular to the line that joins Troy to Delphi, the center of the Greek system of coordinates. That line is at the height of the right-angled triangle, constituting a perpendicular line drawn from the apex, Troy, to the hypotenuse, axis of the drift.

The distance covered during the 9 days adrift is easily calculated. Its square is equal to the sum of the squares of the two sides of the right angle (Pythagorean theorem). Still speaking in terms of geographical degrees, we obtain: $5^2 + 7.5^2 = 81.25$, a figure very close to 9 squared. Now, 9 geographical degrees equal 1,000 kilometers. Hence, Calypso's cave is located some 1,000 kilometers from the west exit of Corryvreckan's strait toward Aquarius; that is, northwest, along a line that forms a 30-degree angle with the north. After some computing, we arrive at the southwestern coast of Iceland as a point defined by:

Latitude 63.40° north
Longitude 17° west

This second calculation of the site of Charybdis and Scylla appears to be much more exact than the first one where Iceland was used for a base. Three discoveries made a more precise figuring possible: the location of the points of departure and arrival on the two axes, north-south and west-east; the remarkable triangle; the direction of the drift that corresponds exactly to one of the axes of the system of zodiacal coordinates.

As a further element, the point of arrival is located on the meridian 17 degrees west, that of Madeira, or the former Aeolia, a key point of the whole itinerary.

For those interested, this is how we reached this arrival point. The coordinates of the point located at sea, at the west exit of Corryvreckan's strait are:

Latitude 56.10° north
Longitude 6° west

For the drift in latitude, one has only to add 7.5 degrees, thus reaching 63.40 degrees. For the drift in longitude, one must change the 5 geographical degrees, or 555 kilometers, to degrees of longitude at the same latitude of 63.40 degrees. For an east-west movement at that latitude, one covers about one degree every 50.5 kilometers. The 555 kilometer longitudinal drift at that latitude covers 11 degrees, yielding a longitude of 6 + 11 = 17 degrees for the arrival point. The coordinates of Calypso's cave would then be:

Latitude 63.40° north
Longitude 17° west

One last coincidence deserves attention. The second key to understanding the text is the speed of the drift; the first one was the ship's speed. The latter was 3.5 degrees for each 24-hour period. Now, the drift in Greece from southern Crete follows a line that is the hypotenuse of the right-angled triangle (formed by the departure point, the city of Troy, and the arrival point). That distance is equal to 9 geographical degrees, or 1,000 kilometers. Since that drift was supposed to last 9 days, the speed of the drift is exactly one land degree for each 24-hour period. That is yet another extraordinary coincidence. Choosing the degree of latitude as a unit of distance measure obviously implies knowledge of the earth's circumference and, consequently, the earth's radius. Such knowledge seems amazing for people living twelve centuries before Christ, in the middle of the Bronze Age. Imagine that they were just as removed from the time of the birth of Christ as we are from the crowning of Charlemagne! And we had not officially admitted the roundness of the Earth until Galileo, less than four centuries ago, proved it.

It is true that classical Greek scholars had already recognized the spherical shape of the earth, for around 235 B.C., Eratosthenes was able to figure the earth's perimeter with less than a 1 per cent margin of error. It is possible that he did not invent the formula he used; he could have simply adapted a new gauge to more ancient methods. The use of the degree of latitude as a unit of measurement of distance, a thousand years earlier, permits us to wonder.

Before trying to resolve the problem, I must compare this fantastic itinerary with what we know today about that remote age. Is this route a plausible one, or does it clash with the archeological information we have?

That problem is on my mind as our *Trident*, taking off from Glasgow, leaves the lochs and the islands behind me. I owe a great deal to Scotland: an exciting search in a wild, yet hospitable, setting; and, above all, a magnificent confirmation of the precision of the *Odyssey*'s message.

I can no longer doubt it: *I am on Ulysses' trail.*

Would a closer scrutiny of the area reveal other precise landmarks, clearly described by Ulysses? The reader is invited to join the adventure and take advantage of a vacation trip to discover on the very spot the various topographical details of Ulysses' itinerary. I shall try to make the search easier and group the landscapes described by Homer according to the countries involved.

At Corfu in Greece you will certainly find the bank of the stream where Nausicaa and her companions washed their clothes. You will also discover the long road across the hill that leads to the Phaeacians' well-protected port on the other side. A view from the city of Antinous at a certain angle reveals on the open sea a small island. Its shape reminds the observer of the ship that brought Ulysses to Ithaca and was then changed into a rock by the god Poseidon who thus wreaked his vengeance on the Phaeacians (Chapter XIII, lines 93 to 184).

Ithaca is the area where many of Homer's descriptions should be easy to verify. First, try to find Ulysses' manor. In Chapter XVI, the movements of the main cast permit certain localizations. The swineherd's hut where Ulysses and Telemachus meet to plan the death of the pretenders must be located at the southern tip of the

island, in the middle of a small circle of hills. The ancient port of
Ithaca must have been at the middle of the island, perhaps at the
very site of the present port. Ulysses' manor was probably at 2.5
kilometers northwest as the bird flies, near a hill. Ship movements in
the port were visible from the porch.

Let us go on to continental Greece. Pylos, on the west coast of
the Peloponnesus, must be located to the north of the present village
of Pylos-KaKovatos, on a hill overlooking a low and sandy coast. But
the most important sites are not in Greece. We will investigate three
areas to trace down Ulysses' itinerary: the Canaries, Ireland, and

Greek vase decorated with representations of Ulysses and Circe. *Photo: Giraudon*

Scotland. In the Canaries, the description of the first island Ulysses reaches is detailed enough in Chapter IX. I quote the pertinent verses in the Appendix. That island can only be Fuerteventura, or Lanzarote. One must find there a "port of safe anchoring" and a "stream at the end of the bay."

In Ireland, there are two regions to explore. The land of the fierce Laestrygonians seems best to correspond to Connemara's mountain mass on the west coast; the pertinent extracts from Chapter X are quoted in the Appendix.

One more landmark to locate here is a "famous port" closed in

on two sides by steep, pointed, and uninterrupted rock walls with overhanging cliffs. The mountains are nearby.

Londonderry and the mouth of the Foyle River at the north of the island are the probable sites that correspond to the Cimmerians' land. We are looking for a section of the river that is accessible with the flow of the rising tide. Investigating the Scottish coast will certainly be an exciting experience.

Barra Island, with its valleys and woods and the sea forming a crown around it, could well be Circe's island. Someone might even find the "Tumulus," tomb of Elphenor the sailor, at the highest point of a promontory.

Sailing southeast from that island, will you find, as I did, the island of the Sirens? The two rocks, one high and smooth, the other with the waves breaking against it? The whirlpool of Charybdis, and Scylla's cave? Yes, I think you will really see all that, as I myself saw it. You should also visit Thrinacia. Exploring it may help you to determine the objectives of Ulysses' voyage. Then you will be convinced, with me, that you are following Ulysses' tracks and have deciphered, at least in part, the meaning of his message.

VI. POSSIBLE OR IMPOSSIBLE?

The means modern technology puts at our disposal strongly tend to make us underestimate the value of ancient techniques for the simple reason that we are no longer capable of using them with the same mastery and effectiveness as did our ancestors who had to use such techniques daily. One may know how to fly a jet plane without having the least idea of how to get around on sea by using the stars as guides. For the past hundred years the frontiers of history have been retreating constantly. Two hundred years ago the Bible was still used to set the date of the origin of the cosmos at 4004 B.C, Today we speak of over five billion years. Each archeological discovery tends to push the origin of human knowledge and skills farther back in time. Only in the last few years, the beginnings of agriculture and of urban civilization have been pushed back several thousand years. The same is true of many other human skills. One wonders where the information transmitted orally through generations actually originated. The first person to express a principle or a theorem in writing is often simply the most recent exponent of a long series of practical observations. We see only that last link, but the origin of specific contents of knowledge and of their first applications could be placed very far back in prehistory. Would that not also apply to navigation, which is our particular concern here?

At the time of Ulysses' voyage, people had long been able to calculate the position of the stars, thanks to Egyptian and Babylonian observations. According to the recent theory of G. Hawkins, professor at Boston University, the circular megalithic monuments at Great Britain's Stonehenge were an astronomical observatory built around

1700 B.C., five hundred years before Ulysses. It would seem, then, that people at that time would have had sufficient knowledge to calculate the position of a ship far away from the coast or to figure the latitude of an island, of a new land. The art of navigating with sails and oars had been known and practiced for more than two thousand years. A third element enters every successful venture of this kind: the sailor's daring, his taste for adventure and discovery. These have always been present.

In view of these three factors, it is no exaggeration to hold that Ulysses' voyage along the suggested route was technically feasible, although actual experiementation would obviously lend more weight to this claim. There seems to be nothing reckless in claiming that, *in view of the astronomical knowledge of the time and the prevailing methods of seafaring by sail and oars, the suggested itinerary is a possible one.* This mere technical possibility, however, does not prove that the *Odyssey* was more than a travel account.

If, on the other hand, we can prove that the Greek audience was able to reconstruct this itinerary from Homer's text, and from that alone, then the *Odyssey* is no longer a mere account but also a message.

What, then, is this secret of the *Odyssey*? A message, hidden in the epic story of a heroic individual, sprinkled with fantastic episodes. And what would the message convey? A series of navigational data: bearings to follow; distances to cover; the relative positions of the stopovers; well-sheltered ports; availability of fresh water and game; desert islands and lands whose people are hostile; important landmarks, such as volcanos, estuaries, rocks, or information on tidal currents, fog, etc. Along with these, the poem conveys some observations more scientific in nature and relating to the length of the day and of tides, the height of the constellations over the horizon, etc.

The story is, indeed, the description of an Atlantic sea route. The route was supposed to remain secret, as was the case with all maritime discoveries throughout history.

The author follows a certain procedure to assure that the exact meaning of the message is available only to the initiated.

First, the data are dispersed throughout the story and shrouded in a mythological tale starring Athene. The listener was supposed to be able to select the actual information, as I myself have done. Only sailors, merchants, pilots, or geographers could have been interested in that aspect of the story and have made the selection.

If the listener was not a Greek, two essential keys to the message in all probability would escape him. He would not know Ithaca's exact topography, the distance from the island of Asteris, the distances separating Ithaca from Pylos or of Corfu. Consequently, he could not know the speed of the ships in the Greek itinerary and transpose it into the Atlantic.

Next, even supposing that a would-be spy cleared the first obstacle, he would run up against a second hurdle: bearings.

The ship's direction is easy enough to figure when the names of the winds are mentioned. But we have seen that this method is used only to indicate the four cardinal points. When the ship sails at an angle to those two main axes, north-south and west-east, one must know the constellation corresponding to the exact bearing and that the bearings are given in a reference system of six axes delimiting altogether six areas, each of 30 degrees. There again, acquaintance with Greece is indispensable since the reference to that system is expressed by way of Ulysses' and Telemachus's stopovers that exactly delimit the areas of 30 degrees, with Delphi as their center.

Finally, the audience had to know the principle of zodiacal projection on the earth, and the correlation between these zodiacal signs and the animals or persons in Greek mythology. Were those furnished with this knowledge able to understand the message? To answer the question, I shall attempt to translate into "clear language" the *Odyssey*'s message. The names of winds and the references to zodiacal signs will be replaced by the real bearings. The days of navigation will be expressed in nautical miles.

After Cape Malea, take the direction that leads beyond Cythera (west). Cover a distance corresponding to nine times 210 miles, or 1,890 miles, arriving at the "continent" (African) at Egypt's latitude (lotus). Leave the coast, and 50 miles out at sea, you arrive at the first island of an archipelago that is very fertile compared to the land previously visited (Fuerteventura).

An island with a well-sheltered port, abounding in water and goats, not too far from another island located west (Ram) with a very high peak and a volcano (Cyclops) that emits stones. Return to the first island. From there, strike a course on Aeolus (Aquarius—30-degrees northwest) to reach an island with steep, bronze-colored banks. This island is located at a distance nine times 210 miles from Ithaca, or 1,890 miles west of Ithaca. After this island, sail six times 210 miles, or 1,260 miles or 21 degrees of latitude, to reach the famous port of the land of Telepylos (faraway port) in the direction of the Bear (She-bear fountain) in relation to the preceding stages. This land—mountainous and wooded, with ports surrounded by perpendicular rocks—is inhabited by giants (northern direction), the fierce Laestrygonians. In the month of June, the days are so long that a man could earn a double salary. Continuing forward in the same direction, with less than 24 hours of sailing (the number of days is not indicated), one arrives at an island. From the highest peak, one can see the ocean forming a crown around the island; its position is in the direction of Sagittarius (Artemis the Archer—30 degrees northeast) in relation to the last point. It is advisable to winter there since the island has a good port.

Leaving at sunrise, at a half-day's sailing south (Boreas wind), about 100 miles, you find an estuary. Using the flow of the tide, one can go up the river (Foyle) and return in a full day's time. That is the Cimmerians' land, often covered with fog. If one leaves in the evening, one can return to the island in one night.

Setting sail during the longest days of the year, follow the Leo-Aquarius axis (Sirens), northwest-southeast with a 30-degree angle in relation to the north. Pass near an island; shortly afterward, two rocks appear. One, smooth and higher than the other, is located north (birds and trees); at its foot, the whirlpool of Charybdis boils over, three times a day. Take the direction of Scylla's cave; its entrance faces west. Immediately after, one cannot help passing the island of the "three teeth" located southeast (direction, Taurus). The whole journey from Aea's can be made in a half day; that is a distance of about 100 miles. If the wind is blowing south and east, the ship must not leave the coast; that means the coast faces southwest-northeast.

For a return with heavy cargo, it is not advised (danger of shipwreck) to go in a southwest direction. Since that bearing is an unlucky one, follow the opposite route, that is, in astrological language, the one perpendicular to it (southeast-northwest), toward the northwest. Pushed by Notus (south wind), the ship will pass by the rocks. The distance to cover now and the direction to take are exactly those of a trip starting at a point between Crete and Libya where land disappears, and a point in the Thesprotians' country, that is, at a day's sailing from Ithaca, about 100 miles north of Ithaca.

One then reaches "faraway Ogygia" with its cold climate. However, the vegetation is varied, watered by fountains that flow in all directions. The island is not inhabited; neither man nor ships are available for returning from there. The presence of the vine (allusion to Dionysus) and owls (Athene) indicate that this island is on the axis northwest-southeast in relation to the preceding point (the rocks). In relation to Olympus, it is located toward the peak neighboring the Pieria chain (northwest); Hermes, to return there, must fly over long stretches of water. This island is located at a high latitude, about $64°$ north, since each night the constellation of the Oxen lightly touches the ocean. Nevertheless, one cannot return from there directly. First, take a southerly direction when leaving the island. In autumn, keep the Great Bear on the left and the Pleiades in front. Since a point exists from which one can (pushed by Zephyr), return to Ithaca in nine days, and since the return trip lasts 17 days, one must sail in a southerly direction for eight days, covering 8 times 210 miles, that is, 1,680 miles, or a latitude of $28°$. Then, nine days of sailing (1,890 miles) lead to Scheria (Corfu). One reaches Scheria by following the Sagittarius axis (northeast 30 degrees). From Scheria, one must leave at sunset to arrive at Ithaca before dawn, at the moment when one still sees the shepherd's star; that is about 10 hours of sailing.

This translation of the message is quite imperfect. I have deliberately omitted many secondary details, but I think it summarizes the essential points.

What precautions to take to keep the secret of this itinerary so that the Phoenicians "abounding in deceit" could not understant the true meaning! That sea route must have been very profitable to the people of Ithaca and Cephalonia; otherwise, they would not have reserved the secret for knowledgeable Greeks, nor would they have taken such care to pass on the legend intact for several hundred years. The poetic from of the tale was useful; the metrical rhythm assured control of the text's transmission. Any error, omission, or modification risked disturbing the poetic harmony. There is little chance of textual deformationa; that is why, even today, we must closely adhere to Ulysses' tale.

Now that there is no longer any doubt of the message's existence, one may question the probability of the contents.

In view of the current state of our historical knowledge, could such a sea route have existed so long ago? To resolve that doubt, I must place myself through imagination at the end of the Bronze Age, in the Mediterranean basin and in Western Europe. I will rethink the voyage in light of our current knowledge of that age.

The Achaeans, a people of Indo-European origin, appeared in Greece around 1800 B.C. They drove out or assimilated a more ancient people related to the Cretans, the Pelasgians. Cretan civilization reached its fullest development around 2500 B.C. Its power was based on commerce, its many cities abounded in wealth. Homer mentions ninety cities! That civilization called Minoan for its most famous king, Minos, and known to us through Greek legends spread throughout the whole eastern Mediterranean.

Toward the west, in Sicily and Spain, archaeologists have found products probably brought there by Cretan sailors. Since that age, a certain unity of civil zation seems to characterize all the places mentioned in Ulysses' itinerary. The sun cult, symbolized by a solar chariot or solar boats had already extended from the Aegean Sea to Scandinavia. The cult of the double axe, or bipennate, was also widespread. Raymond Furon (in his *Manuel de Préhistoire Générale*) writes: "This symbol, along with thunder and lightning, is found in Cnossos' palace in Crete. One finds it in northern Italy, in the Balearics, Spain, Brittany and Scandinavia."

Cretan supremacy of the seas was so complete that Cretan cities were not even fortified. Sir Evans found Minos's palace at Cnossos. Its reconstruction, questioned by some, does show in a striking way the importance of the palace, its complex architecture that inspired the legend of the Minotaur and the Labyrinth; its internal arrangement; the way of life and the distractions of these early heralds of Greek civilization. It is important to ask whether the Cretans, whose exploits date from two to ten centuries before the supposed date of Ulysses' voyage, (twelfth century B.C.) were already able to sail far from their own coasts into the Atlantic.

On maritime discoveries and ancient navigation techniques, we refer to *Histoire de la Navigation* by Pierre Célérier (Presses Universtaires Françaises [P.U.F.]).

History proves that well before our era, great sea voyages were accomplished. Crossings between lands separated by thousands of kilometers of ocean took place almost regularly, without any high-seas navigation equipment.

Observations of the heavens and of the movement of the stars seem to go back to the very first ages. We know, in any case, that certain peoples, like the Egyptians, possessed an extensive and exact astronomical knowledge several thousand years before our time. Navigators used the azimuth of the Sun and the stars at different seasons and at different hours of the day with sufficient approximation to find their way on the seas.

Our school-bred habit of not applying our curiosity much beyond classic Antiquity often prevents us from viewing the enormous stretches of preceding and perhaps equally civilized ages. Yet we have every reason to suppose that periods of civilization have been erased from man's memory; and doubtless, navigation was practiced then as well as during historical times . . .

The possibility that people sailed on the high seas to great distances several centuries before the Achaean age seems to be established without question by specialists in the history of navigation.

Why, then, did the Ancients of classical times not know of this? Because of the simple reason, I believe, that the holders of all that nautical information did not wish to reveal it. In the same book, Pierre Célérier adds:

> The Scandinavian sagas that have reached us often refer to information they do not actually reveal. When they do give details, they seem to be speaking of routine trips . . .
>
> Likewise, it is certain today that fishermen from the French coast frequented Newfoundland's coast several centuries before the official discovery of America. One finds no trace of information about that navigation; they must have jealously guarded the secrets for themselves. We know that lands were known and frequented long before the official date given for their discovery, the main instance being America.
>
> Why could the same phenomenon not occur in a more distant past? The secrecy which surrounded those discoveries should be enough to make the point clear.

In support of this theory, we might quote the recent discovery of a stele on the Brazilian coast. The letters engraved on the stele are unquestionably Phoenician.

The *Odyssey*'s itinerary, then, does not seem improbable in itself, nor is it incompatible with the available methods of navigating the high seas since these go back to an even earlier age.

Let us now return to Greece. The island of Crete seems to have come under Achaean control around 1400 B.C. The palace of Minos is burned down, and several cities are destroyed. But the Achaeans become in fact the Cretans' heirs. They certainly followed the same western routes as did the Cretan sailors. Tablets with so-called Linear B writing, discovered at Pylos and Mycenae, and others discovered in Crete show that these two peoples spoke the same archaic Greek. The decoding of these findings has not yet been completed.

The kings of the house of Achaea called themselves descendants of mythological heroes, or often children of Zeus. According to Greek legend, Zeus was born in one of the caves on Crete's Mount

Ida. These caves have been found and excavated. In *Les fils de Minos*, H. Hariel Courtes comments on the findings. Votive objects bear witness to the cult of Zeus, as do double-edged axes and (bipennates,) a widespread Western symbol of Zeus.

This descent of the Achaean heros from Zeus, himself born on Crete, must mean that the Achaeans considered themselves related to the Cretans. Current translations of the Mycenaean and Cretan tablets seem to confirm this claim.

By some effective means, whatever they may have been, the Achaeans inherited the maritime traditions of the Cretans, even surpassed them by their own distant expeditions. On this subject I quote Gabriel Leroux in *Les civilisations de la Méditerranée* (Presses Universitaires Françaises):

> Even if we cannot say for certain that Cretans frequented the western Mediterranean markets, numerous traces of an Aegean influence there prove that the Mycenaeans did not fear those faraway expeditions. The first stop westward was, no doubt, Corcyre (Corfu). Malta's and Sicily's debt to Aegean influences has already been noted ... The Mycenacans next went to the Aeolian islands to buy [liparite,] then to Sardinia where they sold copper ingots that bore Aegean seals, then to the Balearics, etc. On the Iberian coasts, the designs, jewels, and other objects of Egyptian style, which the Mycenaeans copied for exportation, bring us perhaps to the kingdom of Tartessos ...

We see that our Mycenaeans have already made a great deal of progress along the route later followed by Ulysses. Tartessos in southern Spain, at the mouth of the Guadalquivir, is located on the Atlantic beyond the Pillars of Hercules.

A word about the Pillars of Hercules. They stand for the present Strait of Gibraltar. According to Greek tradition, Heracles (Hercules) opened the strait by pushing back the mountains between the Mediterranean and the Atlantic. The tradition could be an embellished record of Heracles' passage through the strait; he seems to have been one of the first Achaean kings and founder of the Heraclidan dynasty. Since the Mycenaean kings at the time of the Trojan War considered themselves descendants of Heracles, the discovery of the strait would date back to an epoch long before the *Odyssey*, probably two or three centuries earlier. In the legend, Heracles sailed between the Pillars to reach the garden of the Hesperides from which he was to bring back the golden apples. Many commentators think the garden is a reference to the Canaries. We are, in fact, on the ancient gold trail that came up from Senegal and followed a sea route along the African coast.

We are still on the same sea route, and the Canaries mark the second stop in Ulysses' voyage. If the Achaeans really reached the archipelago at that heroic age, which must have been an age of great maritime discoveries since other expeditions, like that of the Golden Fleece, occur at the same time, then it is not unlikely that their descendants in following centuries relied on those first discoveries in their own exploration of the Atlantic Ocean.

According to a theory by Pena Basurto, a Spanish archeologist, the Cretans probably reached Tartessos around 2200 B.C., that is, a thousand years before Ulysses' time. Furthermore, ancient Greek legends indicate that Tangier was founded by Heracles.

Hence, the Aegean world knew the Atlantic gateways well by the time that Agamemnon led the Achaeans on the Trojan expedition. At any rate, by the 12th century B.C., the western Mediterranean had certainly long since been explored by Cretan and Mycenaean ships. It follows that Ulysses: adventures could not reasonably be located in the neighborhood of Sicily and Italy; the latter were only the first stops on an ancient commercial route.

Homer's commentators, among them Bérard (*Dans le sillage d'Ulysse*), deliberately limited themselves to the Mediterranean, refusing from the outset to cross the Strait of Gibraltar. Raymond Furon in his *Manuel de Préhistoire Générale* takes the other side:

> Aegean sailors imported bronze to the Iberian peninsula at the beginning of 2000 B.C. Their stopovers are found in Sicily and Southern Italy.

There seems to be no doubt that the Aegeans had discovered the Atlantic Ocean in remote times.

Evidence of a Mycenaean commercial expansion was found in excavations along the periphery of the Mediterranean. From that age on, Argolis with its cities of Tiryns and Mycenae ruled all of Greece. After 1400 B.C., this hegemony seemed to replace Cretan rule altogether. Excavations reveal luxurious golden and silver jewelry and bronze weapons that fit Homer's accounts perfectly. Gabriel Leroux in *Les premières civilisations de la Méditerranée* (P.U.F.) points out, however, that "Mycenaean art on the whole became vulgarized and industrialized. Workshops sprang up all over the cities and around the palaces. Networks of busy roads covered Greece; maritime connections developed. Large-scale production with simplified manufacturing methods served a wide market."

As in the case of Crete several centuries earlier, this economic expansion of the Mycenaean period was evidently due to increased overseas traffic and booming foreign trade. In that context, what could be the meaning of the events recorded in Homer's first poem, *The Iliad*, which ends with the capture of Troy by the Achaean Confederation?

Gabriel Leroux expresses his opinion:

The Trojans whose art and civilization resembled the Mycenaeans' very closely were fearsome competitors for the markets in Asia Minor. The siege (of Troy) is usually placed between 1193 and 1184 B.C.

With this expedition, the Achaeans in all probability sought to destroy the major obstacle to their expansion in Asia Minor. In fact, after the 12th century, peoples and whole cities were migrating en masse with their gods, wealth and traditions which included many secrets of Cretan civilization preserved through the Mycenaean period.

Schliemann, using Homer's text, located the site of Troy on Hissarlik hill in Turkey. Several years later, in 1874, he started excavating at the site of Mycenae and uncovered palaces and tombs of Achaean princes that date back, it is certain, before the Trojan War.

Troy was perfectly located to control the routes from Europe to Asia and back. Layers have been found representing cities that were destroyed, then rebuilt on top of one another. The most ancient layer dates back to 3000 B.C. Hence, the city the Achaeans besieged and burned was a very old one. The abundance of Trojan objects of bronze, an alloy of copper and tin, lead some writers to suppose that Troy was a tin market.

According to these authors, there are two possible routes to the tin supply—one from beds in northern Iran by way of the plateaus of Asia Minor, the other coming from Bohemia by way of the Danube.

Once the Achaeans had eliminated their main competitors and gained control of the straits leading to the Black Sea, they could have been tempted to expand westward. What do we know of such a drive to the west? Archeologists assure us that the Achaeans had reached Sicily, Sardinia, the Balearic islands, and southern Spain in the preceding centuries. Legend leads us to believe that the Achaeans had been acquainted with the Atlantic gateway, Tartessos, for a long time. Gabriel Leroux, quoted above, tells us: "The Tartessians occupy [Baetic] and Andalusia, the richest regions in Spain. Famous as metal workers and bold sailors, they attracted merchants from all points of the Mediterranean by their reputation for fabulous wealth and by their commerce in silver and tin.

"Their generous hospitality, their energetic and refined civilization, comparable in its imposing luxury to that of the Orient, deeply impressed the Ancients. According to Strabon, their civilization goes back six thousand years. He praises their poems and the rhymed annals preserved by their priests . . ."

It seems that in the following periods the Greeks had forgotten these ancient contacts until the day when Kalaios of Samos, in 630 B.C., pushed by a storm to Tartessos, returned with a very profitable cargo of gold. Ulysses' itinerary avoids Tartessos, following instead the Moroccan coast with a stop at the Canaries.

If the Mycenaeans were clients of the Tartessians, masters of Atlantic commerce, one easily understands why the preferred route avoided Tartessos. The motives of merchants are immutable.

Arielli and de Castro Farinas's work, *Les Iles Canaries*, gives some details of history previous to the official Portuguese discovery:

Since the most distant times, the Canaries had been inhabited by a very industrious white race, the Guanches ... Guanche mummies show that the people were tall, 1.80 meters at least, with blond or brown hair. It is thought that they had blue eyes ...

They lived in natural caves or in huts with roofs made of plants ...

A study of skeletons found at burial sites confirms that the inhabitants were unusually strong, with an almost superhuman vitality and resistance.

... In conclusion, after a first wave of Cro-Magnon men of Euro-African type whose culture is very ancient, other peoples settled the island; they were Mediterraneans of an easterly type, armenoid, slender; others followed later, importing a more advanced culture.

... The Guanches of Tenerife and of Gomera embalmed their dead in the same way as the Egyptians and the Peruvians of pre-Columbian times.

We can easily draw a parallel between the Guanches and Cyclops, except, of course, for the latter's single eye in the middle of the forehead. This text indicates the possibility of ancient contact between the Guanches and the peoples of the Mediterranean. It is interesting to learn that in the year 1341, a Portuguese expedition crossed thirteen islands of the archipelago and found only five of them inhabited, which corresponds to the situation described by Ulysses. Still more impressive is the comparison between Homer's text and that of the Norman navigator, Kean de (Bethencourt,) in his story of the discovery in 1402:

The Canary Islands are seven ... the first, when one comes from Castille, is Lanzarote, a land rich in wheat and animals, especially goats. It would be a good land for grapes and trees, but the plants do not grow because the many grazing cattle destroy everything. There is no fresh water.

Farther, Fuerteventura: it is rich in fresh river water. There are many goats, a few cows, some grapes, vegetables, almond and other trees; it is located three leagues from Lanzarote.

The great Canary is immediately after: a large island, rich in fresh river water, with much sugar cane, corn, wheat, barley, wine, fig trees and many date trees.

Tenerife is next . . . where there is a chain of the highest mountains of the world; upon the peaks, flames appear sometimes as at Mongibel in Sicily.

The presence of goats and fresh water at Fuerteventura is noticed by both navigators.

The flames from the volcano of Tenerife evoke the activity of the largest of the Cyclopes, Polyphemus, son of Poseidon the Earth-shaker.

After a stopover at Madeira, our route takes us to Ireland and Scotland. Could the Mycenaean sailors have wandered that far into the Atlantic? Will archaeological contributions allow us to locate this voyage in relation to what we know of that period of the history of Great Britain?

The British prehistorian Gordon Childe in *De la Préhistoire à l'Histoire* offers a well-supported opinion in favor of commercial relations between the British Isles and the Mediterranean since the middle of 2000 B.C.:

In Mycenaean Greece . . . merchants made substantial profits, and had access to high social standing.

After 1400 B.C., Mycenaean commerce succeeded the Minoan . . . Mycenaeans exported pottery toward Troy, the Southwest coast of Asia Minor, Syria, Egypt, Palestine, Sicily and Italy.

Mycenaean commerce turned toward uncivilized Europe. The pottery reached Macedonia and Sicily, and went farther still. Beads and crockery fashionable in 1400 are found as far as in Southern England. A Grecian-made dagger has been discovered in a Bronze Age mound in Cornwall. In exchange, Mycenaeans imported tin from Cornwall, gold from Ireland and ornaments made in England . . .

Thus from that time the uncivilized lands, including Ireland and Denmark, made a positive contribution to the collective experience of people whose home was the Near East.

It is possible that the Bronze Age civilizations of Western and Central Europe were born of this proven commercial activity; in any case, the contacts favored their development.

As an example, the barbarian aristocrats of southern England and Denmark, grown rich by the commerce with faraway lands, were the sociological and economic counterparts of the Mycenaean leaders. Assuredly, they were poorer and more provincial; but the contacts between the Nordic aristocracy and the wealthy Minoan world probably contributed to the birth of Greece's heroic age.

Hence, there seems to be proof that these trade relations existed at least one or two centuries before Ulysses' voyage. Concerning the relations between Spain and Ireland, Gabriel Leroux affirms about Tartessos:

Contact with the Atlantic countries, especially Ireland, is more certain. That explains the rapid growth of bronze metallurgy, probably introduced from the East, as copper was from 2000 (B.C.) onward. From that time, the Spaniards must have sought not only Galician tin, but also the tin of Cornwall, the famous Cassiteride islands of the Ancients.

Jacques Briard in "*L'Age du Bronze*" (P.U.F.) offers the following confirmation:

In the Early Bronze Age, Ireland knew a very active metallurgical industry . . . Gold was one of the most sought-after Irish products in the Early Bronze Age. It was exported to England and to continental Europe in crescent-shaped, flat sheets called *lunulae, gorgets* or *diademes* . . . Toward the end of the Early Bronze Age, another original Irish product was the ax, flat, or appearing with raised edges, decorated on the flat surfaces as well as along the raised edges with geometric designs, chevrons, diamond shapes, etc. Axes of this type have been found from Western France to Northern Europe. Irish gold continued to be traded in the Middle Bronze Age.

Glass and faience beads, made in the workshops of Tell el Amarna in Egypt and dated 1400 B.C., have been found in England. Finally, on one of the raised stones at Stonehenge, whose circular megalithic monuments date from about 1700 B.C., there is distinguishable an engraved representation of a Mycenaean-type dagger.

For these reasons, the idea of an Achaean sea expedition sailing here at the time of the Trojan War is not far-fetched at all.

That is an idea that I personally do not hesitate to adopt. The search for gold, this notorious motive that draws men to the seas in all ages, could well have been the object of Ulysses' voyage.

Homer, however, for whom Ireland would be the land of the fierce Laestrygonians, does not seem to make this area the end of the voyage. The "famous port" of [Notos] is rather a stopover on the way to Scotland. Ulysses' successors are strongly advised to stay clear of the port, for the people there are anything but friendly. By contrast, Barra Island, is strongly recommended as a base for starting out toward either the northern coast of Ireland, land of the Cimmerians, or Thrinacia, although the sailors would have to beware of the dangers of Charybdis and Scylla.

VII. TIN, GOLD, OR EXPLORATION?

I had occasion to mention earlier that the slaughter of Helios's cattle, whose skins the sailors must have taken, could have meant a search for ingots of precious metal.

Speaking of the Bronze Age, Jacques Briard notes:

> The raw material travels under various forms. In the Mediterranean the ruling Cretans monopolized the copper trade. The stocks of metal were kept in ingots shaped like oxen hides and often bore favorite Cretan emblems such as the double axe. In Sardinia, the island's own ores were used; however, Aegean ingots in the shape of oxen hides show that Aegean prospectors were the ones to introduce the metallurgical techniques there.

Once again, Ulysses seems to be using a code, speaking of oxen hides instead of gold or tin ingots to hide the real objectives of the trip. Such name substitution commonly occurs among people sharing the same subculture; they use countless "slang" words for "money," which they do not wish to mention.

The metal in question could be either tin or gold.

That the Atlantic islands were rich in tin would support the first alternative, according to the text, we might be heading toward the Cassiteride islands . . .

Let us briefly sum up the data relating to this particular problem. At the end of 2000 B.C., bronze was the favorite metal used for household utensils, weapons, door frames, etc. Bronze is an alloy of tin and copper, to which are added varying quantities of less precious elements such as lead. Copper presents no problems for historians, for it is found in several Mediterranean lands. Its very name comes from the island of Cyprus where there were flourishing mines even in Cretan times, previous to the age that concerns us.

Tin, on the other hand, is practically nonexistent in the Mediterranean basin, except in Etruria. Much of the bronze production in those ancient times, especially in Crete and Greece, depended on a very active tin commerce between the producer countries and the Mediterranean. Several ancient authors referred to such a trade.

According to Herodotus, tin ore, *cassiterite*, came from the Cassiteride Islands located far away, north of Spain. Pliny the Elder recalls that tin was obtained from the Atlantic islands and that it was brought in wicker boats covered with hides, the type of boat that was used by the ancient Celts. Aristotle, for his part, traces the adjective "Celtic" to the Greek *cassiteros*. The geographer Strabon, referring to *Posidonius of Apamaca*, states that there are ten Cassiteride Islands from which the tin came. They are located in the high seas, north of the ports of the *Artabres*, La Coruña, in Spanish Galicia, and are all very close to one another. Now, the Hebrides form an archipleago of some ten larger islands, located exactly north of Galicia.

The most detailed report is found in the *Ora Maritima* of Aviennus, a Latin poet. This is what he says about the inhabitants of those islands:

> They all cross the sea in their canoes which are not made of fir or pine but of skins or hides. It takes two days to go from there to the Sacred Island (Ireland) as it used to be called; the island takes up a large portion of the sea and is the home of the Hibernian people. Albion's island is located alongside . . . That is what Himilco the Carthaginian saw with his own eyes, and I am using the Carthaginian annals to retell it . . .

The account is a factual one and the writer gives the source of his information. He specifies, furthermore, that the Carthaginians ruled many cities and towns beyond the Pillars of Hercules. He especially notes Ophiussa, perhaps the Biblical Ophir, from which King Solomon had gold brought three times a year. According to Aviennus, this land was formerly called Oestrymnis; it is located near the

Cassiteride Islands, and its surface area equals that of the Peloponnesus. Now, Ireland is located immediately before the Hebrides, as
one comes from Spain. Its surface area is larger than that of the
Peloponnesus; that is, Oestrymnis could fit into Ireland. Hence,
Oestrymnis could be the land of the Laestrygonians. The two names
do sound somewhat similar.

Diodorus Siculus speaks of the tin route on which Tharsis, or
Tartessos, in southern Spain was an important stopover.

Most historians hold it for a proved fact that trade between the
British Isles and the Mediterranean countries existed toward the end
of 2000 B.C.

The above remarks lend further support to our theory that is now
beginning to take on some flesh. The famous Cassiteride Islands could
be the Scottish Isles and the Hebrides, ancient suppliers of tin and
starting point of the return trip to the Mediterranean. They become,
with Ireland, the goals of Ulysses who is looking for tin needed for
the manufacture of bronze and thus a very valuable and profitable
merchandise. The Greeks must have gotten particular satisfaction in
bypassing their traditional supplier, the city of Tartessos near Cadiz,
which had a monopoly on that trade. The theory would make the
vigorous fight of the Laestrygonians more understandable; they must
have held a key position on the tin route at the western tip of
Ireland. The famous port that Ulysses mentions may have been the
place where the Laestrygonians stocked the ore shipped in from
neighboring islands on small animal-skin boats, such as the ancient
writers have described. Cassiterite, or tin ore, appeared in the shape
of dark pebbles of alluvial origin and were piled up in easily observable lines along the beaches. The ore was smelted on the spot, either
on the islands or in Ireland, in wood-fueled furnaces, then cast into
ingots before being sold. The metal had to be stockpiled in a port to
allow loading on a seagoing ship or fleet. These ships, coming from
the south, could reach that latitude only during the fair season, or
the "long days" as Ulysses calls them. Convoys must have moved
very slowly. These conditions would not warrant more than one
voyage each summer, perhaps one in every two or three years, as the
Bible indicates in the story of Ophir.

The existence of such convoys is not imaginary; we have records of the tin coming from the Cassiteride Islands by the Atlantic. Furthermore, archeological finds have shown that during the second millenium B.C., the European Bronze Age, trade involving mainly metal ingots and amber from the Baltic existed between what are today the coasts of Germany, Great Britain, France, and Spain. The sea was, then, the main trade route as the most economical method of shipping in all ages, particularly at a time when the forest-covered continent offered nothing but rough trails.

The annual arrival and departure of these convoys were doubtless occasions of great festivals, the first of which must have occurred at the June solstice. The numerous dolmens and the megalithic systems in Ireland and in the Scottish Isles served as observatories for fixing the position of the stars, to forecast the arrival of a fleet and determine its departure date.

There are many prehistoric remnants in the Hebrides and Ireland dated around 2500 B.C. The finds, located mostly near the coasts

Charybdis--a bird's-eye view of the whirlpool, with a gull in the foreground.

Photo: author

and on the islands, show an intensive activity in the area involving mainly seafaring and metallurgy. Some authors claim that the first Celtic (Gaelic) invasions from the present Germany hit Ireland and Scotland at about that time. In fact, Gaelic is the language that must be linked with the proper names quoted by Homer in the *Odyssey*.

The part of Ireland reached by Ulysses, the "country of the Laestrygonians," was probably inhabited by the "Oestrygaels" or Western Gaels, which would shed light on the origin of the word, "Laestrygonian." "Aea" may also echo a Gaelic word. The name "Circe," pronounced "Kirke," could refer to a Celtic priestess, from the radical "kirk" meaning church. In the same way, "Cimmerians" reminds one of the phoneme "kimer," which should mean something in Gaelic.

I have already pointed out the resemblance between "Charybdis" and the Gaelic "Corriev" (Corryvreckan) and between "Scylla" and "Cailleach," the she-devil living in Corryvreckan's cave. I realize that these are presumed relations, not proof; but when they are added to

The whirlpool of Corrievreckan, turbulence visible in the center.   *Photo: author*

all the other deductions flowing from the textual analysis, they could tip the scale toward full evidence.

The search for tin was perhaps not the only reason for visiting countries located so far from Greece. Gold could have entered the picture, all the more since the Ireland of that time was an important supplier of gold. With man's perennial fascination for that metal, it is natural to suppose that the country's fame had spread far abroad and that the Cretans and Achaeans wished to see for themselves where their gold came from. Jura, or Thrinacia, which seems to be the destination of the trip, is formed of quartzite sprinkled with auriferous lodes. The name of its main peak, we recall, means "mountain of gold" in Gaelic.

Twenty-five centuries later, gold was still the strongest incentive that accounted for many Portuguese and Spanish maritime discoveries. Furthermore, we are informed in Chapter I of the Odyssey that Ulysses was in contact with bronze and iron merchants before the Trojan War. A commercial motivation would then be a natural one to assume.

It seems also that Ulysses represented for the Achaeans more than a simple merchant or the king of a tiny island. He is often called "crafty," and also foreseeing or "prudent." Foresight is a quality combining keen observation with the ability to forecast the future. The "craftiness" of Ulysses implies intelligence and knowledge. Ulysses displays qualities typical of a scientific bent of mind: observation and deduction. Why not suppose that his expedition had a scientific objective; a venture to those northern latitudes to measure the length of the day, space the tides, fix the position of the constellations. Moreover, commercial concerns are naturally mixed with the scientific, as was the case later on at the time of the great discoveries.

Perhaps the expedition never even took place. Ulysses' adventure could possibly be a convenient way of gathering in a single shape the maritime information accumulated by Achaean sailors on the Atlantic route during several trips over a long period of time. In that case, Ulysses could well be a mythical figure. On further thought, that seems unlikely to me. Ulysses is too much "present," he is involved in too many episodes of the Iliad with real historical people; we know even how many ships and soldiers they had. I can only think that Ulysses really existed.

If Ulysses is not a fictitious hero, one must then admit that his Atlantic expedition to the Canaries, Ireland, Scotland, and Iceland is a real adventure. As for the interpretation of the text, the codes are relatively simple: transferral to the Mediterranean for obtaining the speed of the ship and reference to the stars for directions other than the cardinal points already indicated by the names of the four winds. Just why Telemachus's voyage was of such interest is now clear; it supplies the essential key. Ulysses' lies on his return to Ithaca also make sense in this light: The fictional voyage in the Mediterranean conveys the coordinates of the nine-day drift.

VIII. A SURPRISING PROBLEM

Hence, the expedition did take place. The discoveries were recorded, then translated into a language that would satisfy two conditions: Exclude understanding by anyone who was a stranger to Greek mythology and make it possible for the initiated to retrace precisely Ulysses' route step by step on the actual spots. The Odyssey satisfies both of these conditions. But then a fascinating question immediately comes to mind.

Since navigation days are used as units for measuring distances instead of the actual time spent on the various legs of the expedition, how are we to explain the precision of the distances measured, which the audience had to know if the text was to be interpreted correctly?

It is a real mystery how these Achaeans in the twelfth century B.C. could fix within a few kilometers the relative positions of islands and continents spread over considerable distances or measure the exact position of the island of Madeira in relation both to Greece and Ireland.

The geographical degree as a unit of measure is explained easily enough, for we may suppose that the Achaeans knew the radius of the earth, hence its circumference and its 360th part, the degree. But even using this measure, how were they able to calculate so precisely the distance separating Corryvreckan from Iceland? The areas are far enough removed from one another to rule out step-by-step triangulation. Only on-the-spot astronomical observation could result in exact calculation of the position of the sites on the earthly sphere.

138

Next, let us grant that the latitude of the spot was obtained by measuring the height of the sun at its zenith or of the North Star over the horizon. The problem of longitude still remains to be solved. A glance at maps of only three or four centuries ago, of the sixteenth century, for example, reveals the complexity of the problem. On these maps the relative positions of lands are extremely inaccurate; the errors, especially in longitude, involve thousands of kilometers. It was not until quite recently that, using measurements collected by artificial satellites, we were able to pinpoint the position of some islands in the Pacific with a margin of error of only a few tens of meters.

In the eighteenth century, the accuracy of new clocks made it possible to calculate the sun's delay or approach toward the zenith in relation to a specific site. Only then could longitude be satisfactorily measured.

It is hard to imagine that people three thousand years earlier, uncivilized tribes just emerging from prehistory, could have possessed a more accurate understanding of the earth than the contemporaries of Newton and Pascal, or even eighteenth-century sailors; in 1750, English and Dutch maps differed from each other by as much as 9 degrees in their respective positions for Newfoundland.

. How are we, then, to attribute such knowledge of the earth, such mastery of astronomical and mathematical techniques to those quarrelsome, violent, and greedy Achaeans? We may assume that the Achaeans were taught by the Cretans who certainly carried on foreign trade earlier. The Cretans themselves must have inherited their mathematical and astronomical knowledge from the Egyptians or the Babylonians. Why was this information lost later? Was it lost all at once, or gradually? It appears that the knowledge of a maritime route to Western Europe and Iceland was preserved for several centuries. The Carthaginian Himilco, sailing north from the Strait of Gibraltar around 600 B.C., reaches Ireland and sails even farther. Hence he was following Ulysses' itinerary. Was he aware of that? A little later, Pytheas of Marseille while in Corsica meets some Phoenician immigrants from Tyre. Back in Marseille, he organizes and leads an expedition that crosses Gibraltar and advances toward Ireland, following Himilco's, that is, Ulysses' route. Like the latter, Pytheas takes advantage of a stopover to calculate the length of daylight during the June solstice. Heading farther north, he reaches some islands where the nights are only three hours long. Then, from these islands to others, he counts seven days of sailing. It takes him five more days to reach a land that touches the Arctic circle. Since Pytheas is an astronomer, we can trust him on that point. His "Ultima Thule" is the same as Iceland, the home of Calypso, the north coast of which touches the Arctic circle. He will discover that during the winter solstice there nights last almost twenty-four hours. Once more, a navigator is following the route of Ulysses. It seems unlikely that those expedition leaders would start out without preliminary information about bearings. I cannot help feeling that these three expeditions have a common parent, some old saga passed down from extremely distant times.

In fact, Ulysses does not seem to leave to chance his bearings on his *Odyssey*. He mentions a famous port in the country of the Laestrygonians and reaches Aea without hesitation. However, the drift after Charybdis and Scylla is quite different from the conditions of normal navigation. Was the arrival in Iceland a chance event due to a storm? I do not think so, and I continue to believe that the *Odyssey* is a precise message yielding the secret of an established sea route often used since the European Bronze Age by Mediterranean sailors. The bearings of the lands involved were obtained by on-the-spot astronomical observations. The methods were probably based on the movements of the stars in relation to the constellations. Just what processes, what instruments were used? That question still begs for an answer. Nevertheless, if we admit that the decoded text gives an exact sea route, the *Odyssey* takes on a new dimension not only because it reveals the secret of the northwest route but also because it reveals the heretofore unsuspected level of Achaean scientific knowledge. The *Odyssey* may be more yet than simply a way to transmit information.

Once we assume that the basic keys essential to the understanding of the text are known to the listeners, then reconstruction of the itinerary becomes an exciting task that mobilizes a wide gamut of information from the most varied disciplines: all the branches of mathematics, the measuring of lengths and triangles, the rules of proportionality, trigonometry, astronomy, measuring of time and space, etc. The text recalls technical information also: the arts of building and maneuvering ships. Finally, it teaches history, in the guise of the heroic legends, and geography, through the precise description of the relative positions of islands and continents. It touches on the human sciences, pyschology and law, that are often referred to in Ulysses' conflict with the pretenders after his return to Ithaca. In this way, the *Odyssey* becomes a compendium of the scientific knowledge of the period and a remarkable teaching instrument. It can be compared to a vast case study presented in a way to excite the listeners' imagination and interest.

Within the favorable psychological climate thus created, the text transmits the information acquired by preceding generations. If this interpretation is correct, the *Odyssey* gives us the means of measuring the Achaeans' level of scientific understanding, enabling us to fix, on the curve of European progress, a precise point situated at twelve centuries before Christ. In this hypothesis, the *Iliad* and the *Odyssey*, with their poetic form protecting against errors in transmission, would bring to the descendants of Ulysses not only a summary of information and principles but also an effective teaching tool intended to shape the listeners' mind. The story of an interesting human adventure sparks the listener's imagination, prompting him to search for the sources of information and to crosscheck them methodically. In order to reconstruct the itinerary of Ulysses, the listener has to rediscover for himself the mathematical rules needed for fixing distances and bearings. The main elements of a scientific education were present even during those heroic times. Now, we know that the *Iliad* and the *Odyssey* were, for several centuries, the mainstays of Greek education. In that light, the stupendous expansion of classical Greek culture several centuries later, toward the sixth and fifth centuries B.C., is more comprehensible. But it would seem that by that period the true meaning of the *Odyssey* was lost. Already, toward the eighth century, Homer himself did not know which countries were involved in the *Odyssey*. The scientific information, because of the secret surrounding its transmission to a narrow

Ulysses beset by the sirens, a scene painted on a section of an ancient Greek vase.
Photo: Giraudon

circle, was probably slowly lost. Several years after Ulysses' return, toward the middle of the twelfth century B.C., Greece was hit by the Dorian invasion. The peoples of Ithaca and Cephalonia take their gods and their legends to a refuge in Asia Minor, the present country of Turkey. They handed down from generation to generation the memorized text of the *Iliad* and the *Odyssey*, but the true meaning of the message, hidden in Ulysses' epic and in his mythological adventures, had already escaped them. The initiated few who knew the system of zodiacal coordinates must have been massacred or dispersed in the upheaval. When Homer, toward the eighth century, gathered, compared, and recorded the scattered stories, the true meaning had already been lost for a long time.

IX. ULYSSES' FINAL FATE

In the light of what we now know about Ulysses' voyage, how should we interpret the episodes following his return to Ithaca?

The *Odyssey* lacks a conclusion. Now that I know which route his expedition followed, I cannot help raising some further questions. The twenty-fourth and last chapter does not satisfy me. Too many facts and attitudes remain unexplained.

When, at the end of the chapter, Athene abruptly ends the fight and sends everyone home without resolving the problems, the reader is left feeling uncomfortable. The story should not end like that; the accounts have not been settled. Ulysses has not justified his massacre of the pretenders—an excessive punishment, applied without judgment and chance for appeal. Those who storm Laertes' house to seize Ulysses certainly have not forgiven him the death of their brothers and friends. Several times there is mention of the law of blood that demands retribution or at least the exile of the guilty one and confiscation of his goods. That is precisely the final fate that Tiresias the soothsayer had predicted for Ulysses when our hero consulted him at the country of the ex-Cimmerians. His fate was to be fulfilled after a difficult return trip fraught with dangerous episodes that eventually came true one by one.

As the actors are suddenly dismissed at the end of the twenty-fourth chapter, each side is still holding its basic position. I cannot resist imagining a different ending, a twenty-fifth chapter dealing with Ulysses' trial. Yes, a trial. For an objective list of the important facts shows up Ulysses in an altogether different light. We shall see that in spite of the lack of formal proof, the prosecution's dossier contains a serious presumption of guilt.

To understand Ulysses' personality, we must go back twenty years, to the beginning of the Trojan War. We know that Agamemnon spent more than a month in convincing Ulysses to take part in the Trojan expedition. It is natural to suppose that in view of Ithaca's geographical position, Ulysses was not very enthusiastic about a journey northeast, to the other end of Greece, and that he tried to negotiate some favorable terms for his participation.

The capture of Troy opened the gates to the Black Sea for the Achaeans; it gave them control of the land route from Europe to Asia, across the Bosporus. A successful expedition could only be of benefit, especially to the eastern Greek cities on the Aegean. By contrast, the people of Ithaca and Corfu are so placed as to control the trade coming from the west. It would seem normal under such circumstances that Ulysses should ask the Achaean Federation's support for a western expedition in return for his participation at Troy.

Let us not forget that Ulysses was a merchant. Athene, in order to prompt a new search for Ulysses and bring about Telemachus's departure, appeared in the guise of Mentor, Ulysses' associate in the iron and bronze trade. Later in the *Iliad*, at the Trojan walls, Agamemnon called Ulysses "crafty and greedy". In a battle that the Achaeans lost, the "prudent" Ulysses ran away from the enemy and redeemed himself only by the cunning episode of the famous Trojan horse. On the other hand, he was the one to receive the diplomatic assignments; his negotiating skill, to which lying is not a stranger, was readily recognized. His undeniable competence as a sailor also brought him leadership of the fleet.

The accounts of Ulysses and Nestor, king of Pylos, after the departure for Troy show evident discrepancies. Ulysses claims that the wind pushed him toward the Ciconians' country. Nestor, who accompanied him to the island of Tenedos, says that he saw Ulysses sail for Troy with Agamemnon. Therefore, Ulysses' statements are contradicted by those of other witnesses.

After rounding Cape Malea, Ulysses says that a storm pushed his fleet for nine days beyond Cythera. To say the least, it seems odd that twelve ships, unable to return to Ithaca because of a storm followed by nine days of drifting, should reach the Lotus-eaters' land as a fleet. It seems more likely that Ulysses deliberately led his ships west to carry out his expedition. He might be using the storm as an excuse, hiding from the Phaeacians the fact that the expedition was planned without their knowledge.

Ulysses and Circe, caricatured by the Boetians about 400 B.C. when Ulysses' adventures in the Septentrionales had become a subject for satire. *Photo: Marburg*

After the arrival at the Cyclôpes' land, an episode reveals conclusively that Ulysses is the head of the expedition. The sailors kill some goats and divide the booty equally, except that Ulysses receives an additional part. His position as a leader, then, implies full responsibility for the succeeding events.

Upon leaving the island of Aeolia for the second time, Ulysses does not specify his destination. He heads north without bothering again to use the storm as an excuse. Obviously, he knows where he is going; he speaks of the "famous" port of Notos in the Laestrygonians' country. He does not seem surprised to reach a well-known port. Here his behavior is strange for an expedition leader. Knowing that the port with its narrow entrance is a potential trap, he takes care to moor his own ship outside the bay while allowing his other ships to enter the port. The herald he sends ashore to investigate meets the daughter of the Laestrygonian king. The attack on the ships anchored in the port begins at that moment. Only two men escape the massacre and reach Ulysses' craft lying outside the port. This sad incident shows the extent of his responsibility as a leader. In full knowledge of the risk and against his will, he let his ships enter the harbor. Whether the action was a result of a breakdown in discipline or a tactical error, Ulysses' behavior as an expedition leader is hard to defend.

Having reached his objective, Thrinacia, he explains the loss of his companions by a shipwreck caused by lightning. Only by hanging on to the hull of his mastless ship and leaving his sailors to be carried off by the waves could Ulysses save himself.

Instead of returning directly to Ithaca, Ulysses bypasses it and goes to Corfu and the Phaeacians. In exchange for the detailed account of his adventures, he obtains not only a ship equipped especially for him but also gifts that he hoards in a cave as soon as he reaches Ithaca.

All that attention goes far beyond simple hospitality to the victim of a shipwreck. More likely, the message included in the story was extremely important to the Phaeacians, "friends of the oar." That would explain his welcome and the presents.

Back in Ithaca, Ulysses does not dare to make himself known, even to his friends; he identifies himself only to the faithful swineherd and to his son. To the former, he tells the story of a fictional voyage. He could have recovered his goods in the traditional way, by recourse to the justice of the marketplace assembly, but Ulysses chooses to administer justice himself because he knows that the Ithacan people would not back him. He sets a trap for the suitors and massacres them all without even listening to them. However, after the death of their leader, all are ready to surrender and pay reparations. Ulysses' only answer is to murder them methodically and so bring mourning to every family in Ithaca and the neighboring islands.

Those are the bare facts that a prosecutor might assemble for Ulysses' trial.

Using these facts, the prosecution would then have to build a case that completely and coherently explained Ulysses' actions. Such a dossier is easier now to formulate. Mentor, an associate of Ulysses, knows the latter's plans and intentions, as well as the expedition's secret goal—the search for the tin route. He does not lose hope of seeing him return. For that reason, Mentor encourages Telemachus to investigate. Ulysses, with the complicity of his pilot, leads the ships west on a planned itinerary, one that perhaps the pilot had already covered. Defeated in Ireland by the Laestrygonians, under conditions that were shameful for an expedition leader, Ulysses continues on his way, winters at Barra, and explores Northern Ireland and the Scottish islands the following summer. Once he has reached his goal, he returns home as the only holder of the secret of the tin route, having conveniently rid himself of the last witnesses of his inglorious adventure.

At this stage, Ulysses knows that he would have trouble justifying the loss of his ships and men before his Ithacan compatriots. Furthermore, he would have to share the fruits of his expedition with his associates. He prefers, then, to head for Corfu and, in exchange for some treasure, reveal to the rivals of Ithaca the secret sea route. He carefully conceals the treasure on his arrival in Ithaca simply because he would have difficulty justifying its origin. Ulysses' first account should have been to the landholding families of Ithaca—Zanthus and Dulichion—for they furnished his ships and crew. In addition, the finest men from those families were suitors, camping on his property, awaiting Penelope's decision. In such a situation, Ulysses could not take possession of his goods and reign again over Ithaca.

He knows that the people would not follow him and that a public debate would demand explanations from him. His only option is to kill all of the suitors since they are precisely the ones with a right to ask for an accounting. The people, thus intimidated, would then submit to the law of the strongest. Ulysses knows, furthermore, that his present condition on Ithaca is untenable whether he uses a false identity or his own name. Corfu is not far, and certainly some day a Phaeacian sailor is bound to pass through Ithaca with the true version of his adventures, a very different version from the one the Ithacans have learned from him.

The treasure hidden in a cave could also be found—the island is not overly large. Hence, he must act quickly. He soon finds a pretext, but that would seem far too slight to warrant the drastic punishment he metes out. The suitors courted Penelope, a rich widow; there is nothing more natural. As for the waste of his goods, the suitors have, at most, helped themselves to the products of his estate. Ulysses dares not, then, give them time to ask forgiveness and offer a compensation that any sensible person would have accepted. That is why he kills their leader under their very eyes and turns a deaf ear on their requests for pardon, their offers of reparation. He compounds his crime by killing all of them to the last man.

This summary of a potential prosecutor's case shows that a trial should have been held to enforce the respect due to law. Even all other considerations aside, the leader of an expedition who has lost his ships and crew must appear before a court to explain matters.

Ulysses' attack on his compatriots by surprise and cunning already constitutes an admission of guilt.

For his defense, Ulysses could hardly invent a new story after having already deceived so many people. It is difficult to guess the ancient procedure in such circumstances, except to suppose that Ulysses could only have benefited by holding to the version that the Phaeacians were bound to spread abroad, that is, the same one that has reached us through Homer.

In their verdict, the island's elders on the jury would have remembered the outstanding services of the Trojan hero. This would probably have saved him from the death sentence. Possibly, at his request, they would have agreed to one last favor: that a potential twenty-fifth chapter should never be recited by the epic poets, so that the hero's memory would not be tarnished in the eyes of future generations.

As a final verdict, one can imagine that after confiscation of his goods to indemnify the families of the victims Ulysses would have been exiled for life to a spot as far from the sea as possible. In that way he would not be tempted to pursue new adventures. Thus the predictions of the soothsayer Tiresias would have been fulfilled:

> Thereafter go thy way, taking with thee a shapen oar, till thou shalt come to such men as know not the sea, neither eat meat savored with salt; yea, nor have they knowledge of ships of purple cheek, nor shapen oars which serve for wings to ships . . .
> In the day when another wayfarer shall meet thee and say that thou hast a winnowing fan on thy stout shoulder, even then make fast thy shapen oar in the earth . . . (away) from the sea shall thine own death come . . .

APPENDICES

EVIDENCE FROM THE ODYSSEY

BOOK 1

The gods are meeting on Olympus. Athena, the goddess with the bright eyes, pleads the cause of gallant Ulysses who is held by the spell of the nymph Calypso on the isle of Ogygia. Only Poseidon, god of the sea and Earth-shaker, away on a trip, could possibly oppose the return of Ulysses because of the grudge he bears against him. For, Ulysses in his travels had blinded the giant Polyphemus, the strongest of the Cyclopes, who happened to be Poseidon's son. Zeus who is presiding over the assembly concludes:

"But come, let us here one and all take good counsel as touching his returning, that he may be got home; so shall Poseidon let go his displeasure, for he will in no wise be able to strive alone against all, in spite of all the deathless gods." And Athene answered him:

Let us then speed Hermes the messenger to the isle of Ogygia. There with all speed let him declare to the lady of the braided tresses our unerring counsel, even the return of the patient Ulysses, that so he may come to his home. But as for me I will go to Ithaca that I may rouse his son yet the more, planting night in his heart, to call an assembly of the long-haired Achaeans and speak out to all the wooers who slaughter continually the sheep of his thronging flocks, and his kine with trailing feet and shambling gait. And I will guide him to Sparta and to sandy Pylos to seek tidings of his dear father's return, if peradventure he may hear thereof and that so he may be had in good report among men.

After speaking, Athene goes to Ithaca where she appears to Telemachus in the guise of a rich merchant, Mentes, the leader of the Taphians, "lovers of the oar." Mentes says that he is going abroad with a shipment of shining iron which he wants to exchange for bronze. "And we declare ourselves to be friends one of the other, and of houses friendly, from of old. Nay, if thou wouldest be assured, go ask the old man, the hero Laertes . . ." It is interesting to note that Athene, in order to gain Telemachus's confidence and to make sure that he believes her, does not take on the guise of a beggar or soothsayer, a messenger or a war lord, but appears simply as a merchant with whom Ulysses had business relations. Their very fathers had known each other and often met, no doubt for the same reasons. Thus, the man least likely to awaken Telemachus's suspicions is a trader who, because of his export-import business of iron and bronze, is quite naturally interested in Ulysses' fate and is anxious to see him get home. Mentes himself makes their common interest quite plain a few verses below: "Many a time have we held converse together ere he embarked for Troy." This statement sheds light on Ulysses' occupation before the Trojan War and on his connections. "Tell me who your friends are, and I'll tell you who you are." If the proverb is true, Ulysses appears to be a big-time merchant and ship-outfitter, which explains how he had the financial and technical means needed for equipping and commanding a fleet of twelve ships. Thus, from the very beginning of the story, one may wonder whether this intervention of Mentes, the merchant to whom Telemachus is ready to listen and whose advice he will follow, does not, in a way, define the nature of Ulysses' adventure by implying a commercial motivation. The episode points out, moreover, that the relationship between Telemachus and the pretenders is a rather equivocal one. As Mentes arrives in Ithaca, he finds Telemachus in the company of the pretenders, enjoying himself with them and sharing their games. Yet Homer is careful to report his true state of mind:

"He was sitting with a heavy heart among the wooers, dreaming of his good father, if haply he might come somewhence, and make a scattering of the wooers there throughout the palace, and himself get honor and bear rule among his own possesions."

This situation startles Mentes-Athene:

What feast, nay, what rout is this? What hast thou to do therewith? Is it a clan drinking, or a wedding feast, for here we have no banquet where each man brings his share? In such wise, flown with insolence, do they seem to me to revel wantonly through the house; and well might any man be wroth to see so many deeds of shame.

Who are these pretenders? Their group of over fifty consists of the noblemen and princes of Ithaca and of all the neighboring islands without exception. "They devour and minish the house" and vie for Penelope's hand. Despite the traditional opinion of Homer's commentators, this courting cannot be a legitimate reason for the pretenders' wasting the fortune of Ulysses and invading his house. The explanation must lie elsewhere. A few lines earlier Telemachus has said that he would like to see his father "bear rule among his own possessions." Could that mean that Ulysses has been stripped of his property rights? The mere fact that he is away from home does not justify the actions of the pretenders. Even if we theorize that Ulysses by his absence has de facto relinquished his legal rights, the logical heirs would be his widow and his son. Yet the pretenders are using up the products of his estate with full knowledge of the community and without apparent protest by Penelope and Telemachus. It seems quite strange that a large number of important and responsible people in Ithaca and the neighboring islands should not only tolerate such a situation but take an active part in wasting Ulysses' possessions. Their attitude, which everyone, including Penelope and Telemachus, seems to be taking for granted, is better explained by the theory that Ulysses owed these people money for which they were collecting interest in his absence by using the products of his lands, killing his sheep, and drinking his wine. What rights could these noblemen, neighbors of Ulysses, have to make themselves at home on his property? What could be a conceivable basis for such a right? The explanation is simple enough if we remember the size of Ulysses' fleet. These rich landowners must have gathered ships, crew, and supplies at the start and entrusted them to Ulysses. Book 2 mentions an agreement between the pretenders: if Penelope chooses a new husband, which would imply admittance that Ulysses is gone once and for all, the man would inherit the house while the other pretenders would receive their share of the rest of the estate. This would indicate quite clearly that they have more in mind than simply taking Ulysses' place as Penelope's husband.

Telemachus decides to follow the advice of Mentes and informs the pretenders that he is going to sandy Pylos and Sparta to investigate his father's fate.

BOOK 2

The next day Telemachus gathers the Achaeans on the Agora and complains publicly that the pretenders are ruining his property. Antinous, one of the pretenders, protests violently and accuses Penelope who, he says, keeps deceiving them. He reveals to the assembly the latest trick of Ulysses' wife. She wished to postpone her decision until she finished weaving a veil that was to be the shroud of Laertes, Ulysses' aged father. Now, to gain more time, whatever she weaves in the day, she unravels at night. Telemachus gives up his attempt at convincing the people and asks instead for a fast ship and a crew of twenty to take him to Sparta where he wishes to inquire about his father's return. At this point Mentor, "to whom Ulysses, as he departed in the fleet, had given the charge over all his house," stands up and chides the assembly for its indifference and apathy concerning the behavior of the pretenders. The pretenders in turn make violent accusations that he is trying to rouse the people against them. The assembly then scatters while the pretenders meet again at Ulysses' house to discuss their concern about Telemachus's intentions. Ulysses' son has his old nurse, Eurycleia, gather some supplies. He tells her about his planned trip but makes her promise not to say anything to his mother for two days. Meanwhile Athene takes on the form of Telemachus, finds a ship, and gathers a crew that is supposed to report to the harbor in the evening ready to depart. At sunset she arranges all the gear on the ship, which she moors at the entrance of the port. Then she makes her way to the house of Ulysses, takes on the form of Ulysses' old friend Mentor, and tells Telemachus that the ship is ready to sail. Both of them hurry down to the harbor where the crew is waiting and take the men up to the house to fetch in one trip all the supplies to be loaded on the ship. They sail out with Zephyr and keep running through the night. We are not told the exact hour of sailing, but we might point out here that after sunset Athene covers the distance between the harbor and the house of Ulysses four times. Book 3 informs us of the hour when the ship puts in at Pylos.

BOOK 3

"Now the sun arose and left the lovely mere, speeding to the brazen heaven, to give light to the immortals and to mortal men on the earth, the graingiver, and they reached Pylos, the stablished castle of Neleus." Telemachus and his companions arrive at Pylos at sunrise, after covering some hundred and twenty-five kilometers during the night. They find a friendly reception at the island and are lavishly entertained. Once the visitors have eaten and rested, Nestor, their host and a former companion of Ulysses, finally asks them about the purpose of their trip. Telemachus tells him that he came to inquire about the fate of his father who has disappeared. Nestor then relates the circumstances in which the Achaeans disbanded after Troy. Agamemnon preferred to stay on the spot. Ulysses follows Nestor as far as the island of Tenedos, then sails north again with his companions in order to join Agamemnon. Nestor came directly to Pylos where he arrived in three days. Since then he has heard nothing of Ulysses at all.

Telemachus spends the night at Pylos. On the morning of the fourth day after a religious sacrifice at dawn, he starts out by chariot toward Lacedaemon (Sparta). "So all day long they [the horses] swayed the yoke they bore upon their necks. Now the sun sank and all the ways were darkened. And they came to Pherae." Pherae is situated midway along the course of the Alpheios River. They leave Pherae at dawn to arrive with the setting sun to castle of Menelaus in Sparta. (See map no. 2.)

BOOK 4

The reception once again is a glamorous one. Telemachus admires the luxurious palace of Menelaus: towering halls, gold and amber tableware, embroidered couches, rugs of thick and soft wool ... Telemachus at this point has not yet revealed his identity. The recital of the heroic deeds of his father and the friendship of Menelaus toward Ulysses move him so much that his tears begin to run freely. Helen, the heroine of the *Iliad*, and now the wife of Menelaus, joins the company. They keep discussing the fate of Ulysses. Telemachus's resemblance to his father soon betrays his identity. Helen then tells what she had known of Ulysses and of the schemes he had invented in order to conquer Troy.

Telemachus stays overnight at the palace. In the morning, Menelaus gives him all the information he has concerning Ulysses. He had learned about the fate of the Achaean leaders from Proteus, Poseidon's servant. According to this information, Ulysses is kept on an island by the nymph Calypso without ship or crew. Menelaus invites Telemachus to spend a few days with him, but the young man is anxious to return to Ithaca and turns down the invitation. Meanwhile, the pretenders, still gathered at Ulysses' house, learn about Telemachus's trip and decide to ambush him as he returns in the strait that separates the southern part of Ithaca from the island of Cepholonia. A messenger informs Penelope of the murderous plan of the pretenders. She asks the gods to spare her son, and her prayer will be granted. At this same time a fast ship manned by twenty determined pretenders sails out in the night and stays under cover next to the island of Asteris along the southern coast of Ithaca, lying in wait for Telemachus.

BOOK 5

On the following day, the assembly of the gods on Olympus hears Athene once more plead Ulysses' cause and tell her fellow gods about the dangers threatening Telemachus. Zeus, in a quick decision, dispatches his messenger Hermes to order Calypso not to retain Ulysses any longer. Hermes takes off from Mt. Olympus and flies over the

Pieria mountain range situated to the northwest of the gathering place of the gods. He covers great distances, flies across the sea, and eventually reaches a far-distant island and Calypso's cave, which is heated by a great fire. Hermes relays to her the message: "Twas Zeus that bade me come hither, by no will of mine; nay, who of his free will would speed over such a wondrous space of brine, whereby is no city of mortals that do sacrifice to the gods, and offer choice hecatombs."

According to this information, the island is deserted. Its climate is harsh, for it is still autumn (which we learn a few lines farther), yet a great fire is already burning in the cave. Homer, however, add these details: "And fountains four set orderly were running with clear water, hard by one another, turned each to his own course. And all around soft meadows bloomed of violets and parsley." Having heard Zeus's will, Calypso protests, but eventually complies with the command. She criticizes the jealousy of the gods that makes them so cruel; they refuse to allow that a goddess mingle with men. She promises nevertheless to "be forward to put this in his mind, and will hide nought, that all unharmed he may come to his own country."

When Hermes takes off again, Calypso goes to find Ulysses who is sitting on the seashore weeping sadly and staring endlessly at the open sea, "for the nymph no more found favor in his sight." She tells him the good news that he is free to go, giving him also instructions on building a craft out of twenty tree trunks and fixing it with mast and bridge. Four days later, after spending a last night with the nymph, Ulysses hoists his sails and puts to sea with a favorable wind. He steers the craft by the helm he is holding firmly in his hand. Since "sleep did not fall on his eyelids," he must be sailing day and night.

> He viewed the Pleiada and Bootes, that setteth late, and the Bear, which they likewise call the Wain, which turneth ever in one place, and keepeth watch upon Orion, and alone hath no part in the baths of Ocean. This star, Calypso, the fair goddess, bade him to keep ever on the left as he traversed the deep. Ten days and seven he sailed traversing the deep, and on the eighteenth day appeared the shadowy hills of the land of the Phaeacians . . .

The *Odyssey* calls this land the island of Scheria, which the ancients identified with (Corcyre,) that is, Corfu. Verse 204 in Book 6 indicates that the land is indeed an island. Several commentators of the *Odyssey* took the trouble to investigate on the spot some of the details of the text that allow the identification that today is generally accepted.

As he is ready to land, Ulysses once more is a victim of the vengeance of Poseidon who is aware of his arrival and stirs up a storm on the sea. The craft turns over and breaks up. After two days of struggle in the water, Ulysses finally comes ashore at the mouth of a river. He is completely exhausted and falls asleep in the woods. Let us call attention here to the distance he covered since having left Ogygia. He has been sailing through seventeen days and nights before he arrives near Scheria.

BOOK 6

Nausicaa, daughter of the Phaeacian King Alcinous, receives in her sleep Athene's advice to leave in the morning and take all her laundry to the washingtanks. She is told to go by carriage since the washingtanks "are a great way off the town." These "tanks" are actually shallow basins on the banks of the river where it meets the sea and where Ulysses happens to be sleeping. V. Berard, author of *Dans le sillage d'Ulysse*, and, later, Jacques Boulenger have reconstructed on the very spot the route followed by Nausicaa. The princess and her companions finish washing the laundry, spread the garments on the gravel, then begin to play ball along the shore. As the ball misses its aim, they let out a loud cry and awaken Ulysses who suddenly appears stark naked before the eyes of the terrified girls. Only Nausicaa has the courage to listen to him attentively. She feeds him, lends him some clothes, and decides to drive him to the town, to her father. She must be fascinated by this strange apparition, for she tells her girlfriends: "Would that such an one might be called my husband, dwelling here, and that it might please him here to abide!"

Ulysses probably came ashore along the west or north coast of the island, which he must cross to reach the city of the Phaeacians located along the east coast, with "a fair haven on either side of the

town, and narrow is the entrance." Nausicaa's chatter contains valuable information on what these people do and how they make a
living. "There men look to the gear of the black ships, hawsers and
sails, and there they fine down the oars. For the Phaeacians care not
for bow nor quiver, but for masts, and oars of ships, and gallant
barques, wherein rejoicing they cross the grey sea." The geographical
position of Corfu, which is situated at the western end of Greece and
guards the entrance to the Adriatic Sea at the closest point to
southern Italy, seems to account fairly well for the interest of the
Phaeacians in seafaring. Corfu was, then, in all probability the last
stop in Ulysses' voyage.

BOOK 7

Ulysses leaves Nausicaa as they arrive at the city gates, for he wishes
to save her from malicious gossip. He alights from the carriage at
sunset and waits in a growth next to the town, leaving Nausicaa
enough time to reach the castle of her father. As he asks his way, he
admits that he is a stranger and does not know anybody in town.
The people of the island "do not gladly suffer strangers, nor lovingly
entreat whoso cometh from a strange land. They trust to the speed
of their swift ships, wherewith they cross the great gulf . . . Their
ships are swift as the flight of a bird, or as a thought."

Ulysses "marvelled at the havens and the gallant ships, yea at the
places of assembly of the heroes, and the long high walls crowned
with palisades, a marvel to behold." The account of the riches of
Alcinous' dwelling may be somewhat exaggerated. "Golden were the
doors that closed in the good house. Silver were the door-posts that
were set on the brazen threshold . . ." "Golden hounds and silver"
guard the entrance. The personnel of the royal household come alive
before our eyes and we see with an amazing clarity of detail these
Bronze Age people as they scurry back and forth:

> . . . Some grind the yellow grain on the millstone, and others
> weave webs and turn the yarn as they sit, restless as the leaves of
> the tall poplar tree: and the soft olive oil drops off that linen, so
> closely it is woven. For as the Phaeacian men are skilled beyond

all others in driving a swift ship upon the deep, even so are the women the most cunning at the loom.

Next comes an account of the orchard and of the fruit that is available all the year round. There is also a flourishing vineyard where "harvesters were gathering grapes while others were treading them." This last remarks indicates that Ulysses' homecoming must take place in the fall.

Alcinous receives him with great friendship, wines and dines him, then offers to take him home to his people the following day. Before retiring for the night, Ulysses tells his hosts about his stay at Calypso's island and his adventurous return.

BOOK 8

At dawn on the following day, Alcinous summons his Phaeacians to the marketplace to introduce Ulysses and arrange for fitting the ship that will take him to Ithaca. The fifty-two young men selected for the mission ready the ship. Then everybody gathers in the castle for a great celebration. A bard sings of the heroic deeds of the Achaeans under the walls of Troy. Ulysses is so moved by this account that he can hardly suppress his tears. Alcinous invites all his guests to take part in sports contests: boxing, wrestling, a foot race, junping, etc. One of the Phaeacians provokes Ulysses by saying that he looks more like a merchant than an athlete. Ulysses meets the challenge forced upon him, picks up a weight, and throws it far beyond the marks of his opponents. The feast goes on, and a harper sings of the mythical loves of Aphrodite and Ares. Ulysses tells his host that he is truly amazed at the Phaeacians' great skill at organizing games, singing, and dancing. In return for the compliment, Alcinous invites his noblemen to gather presents for Ulysses to take along in a coffer on the ship.

At sunset the maids bathe Ulysses in warm water and shower their attention on him. Then he sees Nausicaa and promises her privately to say a prayer for her every day since she saved his life. The celebrations start again, and an inspired minstrel sings the story of the wooden horse at Troy that the enemy itself dragged into the city. Ulysses and his soldiers, hidden inside the Horse, thus pene--

trated the town and eventually destroyed it. The memory of these events again moves Ulysses to a point that tears start running from his eyes. Alcinous notices this and asks him no longer to hide his identity but to speak out and tell where he came from, what countries and cities he visited on his voyage.

BOOK 9

The next four books contain the true story of the voyage of Ulysses who is so moved by the minstrel's song, by the warm hospitality of Alcinous, and perhaps by the rich presents, that he cannot resist the request. From this point on, one must read the story with great attention, for the account of the actual trip contains the essential elements of the mystery of the *Odyssey*, the itinerary of Ulysses that has been the subject of a great deal of study and controversy. Our hero's taste for piracy is well in evidence from the very beginning of the recital. No sooner does he leave Troy than he attacks the city of Ismalos in the Aegean Sea, at the northeast part of the island of Thesos. The Cicones, as the local people are called, return in force at the very moment when the Achaeans, paying no heed to the advice of the prudent Ulysses, celebrate their victory with plenty of wine. The Cicones "who were skilled to fight with men from chariots" throw Ulysses' companions back into the sea with some losses.

A strong north wind drives the ships south. As Ulysses is rounding Cape Malea, that is, the southeast tip of the Peloponnesus, currents and wind push him off course beyond the island of Cythera. To this point the itinerary of Ulysses is simple enough and easy to chart on a map of the eastern Mediterranean sea and Greece. (See map No. 6.)

From here on, however, things get less clear, and interpretations begin to differ widely.

> Thence for nine whole days was I borne by ruinous winds over the teeming deep; but on the tenth day we set foot on the land of the lotuseaters, who eat a flowery food. So we stepped ashore and drew water, and straightway my company took their midday meal by the swift ships.

In the traditional opinion, the island of the Lotus-eaters is the same as the island of Djerba in front of the gulf of Habes along the Tunisian coast, that is, at 1,200 kilometers to the west of Cythera. This interpretation is questionable on two accounts. First, Ulysses speaks of a *continent*, not of an island, and on this very topic his vocabulary is always very precise. In any event, no interpretation may be stretched to the point of taking "continent" for an "island." As a second reason, the distance covered seems very little for ships driven by a storm for nine days and nights. As low a speed as five or six knots would, in fact, yield a distance of about 250 kilometers for every twenty-four hours, or over 2,000 kilometers in nine days.

During this day spent at the Lotus-eaters, some of the sailors taste the lotus, which weakens their will to return so much that Ulysses has to take them back to the ships by force.

They set sail immediately, and following their route they eventually arrive at the land of the Cyclopes.

Things spring for them in plenty, unsown and untilled, wheat, and barley, and vines, which bear great clusters of the juice of the grape, and the rain of Zeus gives them increase ... A waste isle stretching without the harbour of the land of the Cyclopes neither nigh at hand nor yet afar off, a woodland isle, wherein are wild goats unnumbered, for no path of men scares them, nor do hunters resort thither who suffer hardships in the wood. Bereaved of men, the island feeds only the bleating goats. For the Cyclopes have no ships with red cheeks, nor craftsmen who would know the art of building these well-bridged ships ... Such men would have profited by an island so rich in assets. The soil is far from being barren, for all fruits grow there in their proper season. All along the shores of the gray sea there are well-watered meadows with soft soil where vineyards could produce their fruit endlessly; the soil is smooth ... there is also a harbor with safe mooring where no anchors are needed; no rocks to throw from the prow, or cables to tie to the stern; once the ship is beached, one may stay there until the sailors' mood prompts them to put to sea again with the good winds. Deep in the harbor sweet water is running abundantly from a cave and poplars are growing all around. That is where we came ashore, a god was guiding us through the dark night. We could not see a thing.*

I felt that this passage deserved being quoted in its entirety. It is a good example of the meticulous care with which Homer describes topographical details for the benefit of navigators. The text truly sounds like a maritime guide covering every essential point: anchorage, fresh water, availability of supplies on the island, possibilities in the event of future colonization.

The sailors kill some goats for fresh meat and drink their red wine out of the amphorae while watching the smoke rise from the distant land of the Cyclopes. On the next day Ulysses puts out on the gray sea and sails toward the Cyclopes' land, which is covered with pine and oak forests.

Ulysses and his crew suddenly spot a monstrous giant in front of them. The creature looks like a tree-covered mountain peak somewhat isolated from the rest of the highland. Polyphemus the giant locks them in his cave. Ulysses manages to save himself and his men by getting the monster drunk with red wine and blinding him with a sapling of wood hardened in the fire. As he flees on his ship, he cannot resist the temptation to mock the giant. The Cyclops throws huge rocks in the suspected direction of the ship; some fall not too far away. Since Ulysses has named himself, the giant, son of Poseidon the Earth-shaker, begs his father to heap misfortune upon Ulysses that "late may he come in evil case, with the loss of all his company, in the ship of strangers . . ." Ulysses returns within the same day to the island where the other ships are waiting and spends the night there. They throw off the moorings the next day at dawn and get on their way. They "smote the grey sea water with their oars."

Several commentators of Homer see in the Cyclops a personification of a volcano, the single eye being a symbol of the crater. The rocks thrown into the sea by the Cyclops seem a rather faithful image of a volcanic eruption in which lava and solid matter thrown from the crater by underground explosions fall into the water. Some authors thus place the land of the Cyclopes at Etna in Sicily, while others, such as V. Bérard, opt for the bay of Naples and Vesuvius where the neighboring island of Capri would be identified as the island of the Goats, with an abundant supply of fresh meat for Ulysses' crew. As for the Etna theory, there is no island at all in the area. In the case of Capri, the rough and mountainous configuration of the island bears no resemblance whatever to the very precise account given by Ulysses. One would search in vain for "well-watered meadows all along the shores, with soft and smooth soil . . ."

BOOK 10

The expedition arrives at the island of Aeolia which ia "a floating island, and all about it is a wall of bronze unbroken, and the cliff runs up sheer from the sea." Traditional commentators of Homer's text are positive that the island of Aeolia is the same as Stromboli in the Aeolian islands. The conclusions seem evident if we are satisfied by the similarity in name. In actual fact, the similarity does not mean much since the islands may have gained their name at a later age. Ulysses finds friendly reception with King Aeolus who listens to his story of Troy and then asks Ulysses to get ready for his trip home. He locks the contrary winds in a skin that he fastens to the inside of the ship, then sends Zephir to push the fleet toward Ithaca. "For nine whole days we sailed by night and day continually." On the tenth day, they arrive in sight of Ithaca. The companions of Ulysses are both curious and envious, and taking advantage of Ulysses' sleep, they open the skin at the bottom of the ship. The closed-in winds escape, and "the vessels were driven by the evil storm-wind back to the isle of Aeolia." This time the reception is quite different. Aeolus is now convinced that the misfortunes of Ulysses show his disgrace with the blessed gods and orders him off the island.

Ulysses continues the story:

> For the space of six days we sailed by night and day continually, and on the seventh we came to the steep stronghold of Lamos, Telepylos of the Laestrygonians, where herdsman hails herdsman as he drives in his flock, and the other who drives forth answers the call. There might a sleepless man have earned a double wage, the one as neat-herd, the other shepherding white flocks: so near are the outgoings of the night and of the day. Thither when we

had come to the fair haven, whereabout on both sides goes one steep cliff unbroken, and jutting headlands over against each other stretching forth at the mouth of the harbor, and strait is the entrance; thereinto all the others steered their curved ships. Now the vessels were bound within the hollow harbors each hard by the other, for no wave ever swelled within it, great or small, but there was a bright calm all around. But I alone moored my dark ship without the harbor, at the uttermost point thereof, and made fast the hawser to a rock.

The sheer cliffs of Bonifacio have tempted some authors to locate the Laestrygonians' country in that area, more precisely at Porto Pozzo in Northern Sardinia. The giant Laestrygonians flock upon the rocks from every side and attack the Achaeans, hurdling huge rocks from the top and destroying the ships. The only craft to escape the massacre is Ulysses', which steers "away from the beetling rocks" just in time. He evidently owes his safety to having moored his ship outside the harbor, a feat typical of "prudent" Ulysses.

They sail on and eventually come "to the isle of Aea," the home of the goddess Circe, and put in at "the sheltering haven." The men spend two days ashore gathering strength. On the third day, Ulysses climbs upon a rocky hilltop and locates the house of Circe by a column of smoke rising in front of him across the oak forest. The scouting party he sends ahead finds Circe's manor, a house built of polished stone on a clearing in the valley. Circe is friendly to them, treats them to drink and food, but then mixes some drug with their drink and changes them into swine, figuratively, of course. The head of the scouts who is suspicious and wise is the only one not to share the fate of his fellows. He runs back to Ulysses who has remained on the shore with the rest of the crew. Ulysses decides to see Circe personally and free his men. On his way he luckily meets Hermes who gives him and antidote to counter the evil magic of Circe. Hermes also tells him that he should threaten Circe who in her fright would offer him to share her bed. Ulysses would be wise not to refuse the offer if he wanted to free his companions. Hermes adds: "Command her to swear a mighty oath by the blessed gods, that she will plan nought else of mischief to thine own hurt, unman you when you are naked and make you a weakling." The events take place as Hermes predicted. Ulysses and Circe understand each other, the men are freed, and everybody enjoys the great feast the goddess offers them. The reception must have been quite warm, for Ulysses and his crew remain on the island for a whole year until the "long days" return in their annual cycle.

Where is the island of Circe located? The commentators have a ready answer to this question. There exists, in fact, a Monte Circeo on the Italian coast to the southeast of Rome. It is not an island, of course. But let that not be an obstacle; one can imagine that at the time of the *Odyssey* Monte Circeo was detached from the mainland. At any rate, with the return of the "long days," Ulysses' friends remind him that it is time for him to see the land of his fathers. Ulysses agrees and informs Circe of their intention to take to the sea again. Circe has no objections to Ulysses' and his companions' departing; she is even willing to help them by her advice. She suggests, however, that Ulysses should first take a trip to the land of the dead, to the home of Hades and Persephone, to conjure up the dead. "North Wind will bear thy vessel on her way. But when thou hast now sailed in thy ship across the stream Oceanus, where is a waste shore and the grove of Persephone, even tall poplar trees and willows that shed their fruit before the season . . ."

Ulysses is supposed to beach his ship by a river and conjure up the soul of Theban Tiresias who will advise him on the route to follow on the home journey to Ithaca.

At dawn Ulysses wakes his men to go down to the beach and hoist the sails. One of them, heavy with the wine they drank the night before, has been sleeping on the rooftop. He misses the ladder, falls down, and breaks his spine.

"His spirit went down to the house of Hades." The poor fellow certainly took a shortcut to join his friends at the next stop on the trip.

BOOK 11

The ship pulls away and runs with the favorable rear wind.

And all day long her sails were stretched in her seafaring; and the sun sank and all the ways were darkened. She came to the limits of the world, to the deep-flowing Oceanus. There is the land and the city of the Cimmerians, shrouded in mist and cloud . . . Thither we came, and ran the ship ashore and took out the sheep; but for our part we held on our way along the stream of Oceanus, till we came to the place which Circe had declared to us.

Ulysses conjures up the dead and receives from Teiresias some useful advice for his home trip: he must first visit the island of Trident, but he must be careful not to touch the sacred cattle of Helios which graze on the island or else he will lose all his men and will greatly delay his own homecoming. He is also told that he should give a solemn burial to the young sailor who on that very morning was accidentally killed at the house of Circe. Ulysses then witnesses the apparition of men and women, all the main characters of Greek mythology, heroes and kings.

Finally he orders his men to take off. "And the wave of the flood bore the barque down the stream of Oceanus, we rowing first, and afterwards the fair wind was our convoy." Commentators have found a simple solution to the problem of locating this episode: They give up every attempt at localization and are satisfied by the theory that this whole trip to the land of the dead is a purely imaginary one. There have been some, however, who propose the area of Vesuvius as a possible site.

BOOK 12

By night Ulysses is back to the island of Circe. In the morning his men build a pyre, incinerate the body of the young sailor, Elphenor, and bury the ashes along with his weapons. On the top of a hill and over the grave they raise a barrow with a pillar, setting the man's oar vertically into the mound over the tomb. "Now all that task we finished . . ." says Ulysses. Circe and her maids are still full of solicitude for Ulysses and his men, invite them to another great feast, and are anxious to add further precisions to the advice of Teiresias on the route to follow. When Circe is alone with Ulysses in the evening, she tells him about the dangers awaiting him on the trip and what he should do to avoid them. He should not listen to the appeal of the Sirens. After filling the ears of his men with wax so that they do not hear the Sirens' song, he should have himself bound to the mast hands and feet if he wishes to hear the Sirens without risking to yield to their temptation.

After that he can choose between two alternate routes.

On the one side there are beetling rocks, and against them the great wave roars of dark-eyed Amphitrite ... On the other part are two rocks, whereof the one reaches with sharp peak to the wide heaven, and a dark cloud encompasses it ... The rock is smooth and sheer, as it were polished. And in the midst of the cliff is a dim cave turned to Erebus ... whereby ye shall even steer your hollow ship. Not with an arrow from a bow might a man in his strength reach from his hollow ship into that deep cave. And therein dwelleth Scylla, yelping teribly. Her voice indeed is no greater that the voice of a new-born whelp, but a dreadful monster is she ... But that other cliff, Odysseus, thou shalt note, lying lower ... Thou couldest send an arrow across. Beneath it might Charybdis sucks down black water, for thrice a day she spouts it forth, and thrice a day she sucks it down in terrible wise. Never mayest thou be there when she sucks the water ... and swiftly drawing nigh to Scylla's rock drive the ship past ... Then thou shalt come unto the isle of Thrinacia; there are the many kine of Helios and his brave flocks feeding ... If thou doest these no hurt, being heedful of thy return, truly ye may even yet reach Ithaca, albeit in evil case. But if thou hurtest them, I foreshow ruin for thy ship and for thy men ... Late shalt thou return in evil plight with the loss of all thy company.

Ulysses sets sail at dawn, pushed by a fair wind. "Our good ship quickly came to the island of the Sirens." They escape from the danger by following to the letter Circe's recommendations and taking all the precautions.

As soon as we left that isle, thereafter presently I saw smoke and a great wave, and heard the sea roaring. ... Helmsman, thus I charge thee ... keep the ship well away from this smoke and from the wave and hug the rocks ... Next we began to sail up the narrow strait. For on the one hand lay Scylla, and on the other mighty Charybdis in terrible wise sucked down the salt sea water. ... Toward her, then, we looked fearing destruction; but Scylla meanwhile caught from out my hollow ship six of my company ... Thereafter we soon came to the fair island of the god; where were ... the brave flocks of Helios Hyperion.

Mindful of the advice of both Circe and Teiresias, Ulysses wants to skirt the island without coming ashore. It is getting late in the day, though, and the men are so weary that they are in favor of stopping for the night. Ulysses makes them swear that they would not touch the sacred cattle and eat nothing but the provisions Circe gave them. The men swear that they would not kill the divine beasts.

We stayed our well-builded ship in the hollow harbour near to a well of sweet water, and my company went forth from out the ship and deftly got ready supper ... When it was the third watch of the night, Zeus the cloud-gatherer roused against them an angry wind with wondrous tempest, and shrouded in clouds land and sea alike.

The wind keeps blowing for a whole month, always from the south or the east, pinning Ulysses on the island with dwindling supplies. "Hunger gnawed at their belly." His men can no longer take it and are ready to brave the wrath of Helios rather than starving to death. While Ulysses is asleep, they butcher the cattle, offer sacrifices to the gods in the hope of appeasing them, and organize a huge barbecue party. The smoke and smell alert Ulysses. Too late; the massacre of the sacred cattle is an accomplished fact. Zeus promises Helios to punish the guilty and to strike Ulysses' ship by lightning. When the storms lifts a while later and the men decide to take to the sea again, we are not surprised to hear Ulysses tell of the shipwreck of his companions. "The ship reeled all over, being stricken by the bolt of Zeus, and was filled with sulphur, and lo, my company fell from out the vessel. Like sea-gulls they were borne round the black ship upon the billows ...

Ulysses hangs on to the wreckage of the overturned ship.

Swiftly withal the South Wind came, bringing sorrow to my soul, that so I might again measure back that space of sea, the way to deadly Charybdis. All the night I was borne, but with the rising of the sun I came to the rock of Scylla, and to dread Charybdis. Now she had sucked down her salt sea water [and the wreckage of the ship] . . . Steadfast I clung till she should spew forth mast and keel again; and late they came to my desire. At the hour when a man rises up from the assembly and goes to supper, one who judges the many quarrels of young men that seek him for law, at that same hour those timbers came forth to view from out Charybdis. And I let myself drop down hands and feet, and plunged heavily in the midst of the waters beyond the long timbers, and sitting on these I rowed hard with my hands. But the father of gods and men suffered me no more to behold Scylla . . . Thence for nine days I was borne, and on the tenth night the gods brought me nigh to the isle of Ogygia, where dwells Calypso . . .

All of the classical commentators place Charybdis and Scylla in the Strait of Messina, which separates Sicily from the nose of the Italian boot. Before reaching the reefs Ulysses is supposed to have passed by the island of the Sirens, which some authors insits on identifying with Corfu, although Corfu is obviously too far away. From the island of the Sirens, Ulysses reaches Scylla and Charybdis in a short time, and on that very same day he arrives before the island of Thrinacia, or the "three points." The text describes the area of Scylla and Charybdis with such detail that in the event of doubtful localization in physical survey of the spot should make positive identification possible. The Messina area does not seem to have fully satisfied the various authors since the discussion still goes on. There is little doubt, in fact, that any one continuing to look in this area for the famous sites that are described with such precision would be wasting his time. He simply would not find them . . . and for good reasons.

All of the passages quoted above present a landscape that bears no resemblence at all to the Mediterranean shores. Ulysses is navigating on very rough seas, and as the tall waves hit the smooth walls of the cliffs that fall vertically into the sea, the spray wets the rock to great heights. The mountaintops are shrouded in mist. Finally, the phenomenon of Charybdis that occurs three times a day when the days are the longest is a well-known one. It is brought about by strong tidal currents mixed with swirtls, and the event occurs with every high and low tide, that is, every six hours. As for Scylla, the cave is a deep opening on the rock at the level of the water. The waves that penetrate the cave must create a moaning sound that reminds the observer of the den of some monster. Neither does Ulysses speak of a strait but of two islands. After the classical theory, the island of Thrinacia could be nothing else than Sicily. After the nine-day drift, however, most commentators are at a complete loss to identify the island of Ogygia, home of Calypso. Since the island must be at seventeen days of sailing, that is, very far from Ithaca, some authors would have Ulysses drift westward toward the Strait of Gibraltar.

Book 12 is the last chapter of the story that Ulysses is telling the Phaeacians in the main hall of Alcinous's castle. He has already told his host the episode of his return from the island of Ogygia soon after he arrived at the land of the Phaeacians. I have thus all the main data of Ulysses' voyage, especially with the elements contained in the last three books that I found necessary to quote in fair detail. We can now afford to sum up the following chapters rather briefly, pointing out the main line of the action and mentioning the episodes that may provide some indirect clues for the understanding of Ulysses' voyage.

BOOK 13

The Phaeacians have been following Ulysses' story with great attention. Alcinous thanks the storyteller and invites all members of the audience to express their gratitude by offering Ulysses a tripod and a cauldron as gifts. Then everybody retires for the night. The gifts, of solid bronze, are loaded on the ship at dawn, after which everybody gathers once more at the castle of Alcinous for a last celebration. "But Ulysses would ever turn his head toward the splendour of the sun, as one fain to hasten his setting; for verily he was most eager to return ... so welcome was the sinking of the sunlight to Odysseus."

He stands up and says good-bye to his hosts, reciting the usual phrases to wish them every happiness and prosperity.

Our hero boards the ship and falls asleep as the oarsmen "leant backwards and tossed the sea water with the oar blade ... she and [the ship] ran ever surely on her way ... So when the star came up, that is brightest of all, and goes ever heralding the light of early Dawn, even then did the sea-faring ship draw nigh the island [of Ithaca]."

The Phaeacians put Ulysses and the gifts ashore near a cave. Poseidon, who still hates Ulysses, asks Zeus to punish the Phaeacians who helped Ulysses, that they may "cease from giving escort to men." Zeus's suggestion is to change the ship of the Phaeacians into a rock when on their return they come in view of the city. The idea is carried out. Ulysses wakes up but does not recognize his home island, for Athene has spread a thick fog around him to prevent his being recognized right away. Some authors think to have found the "well-sheltered haven" on Ithaca, as well as the cave where the Phaeacians have put the sleeping Ulysses ashore.

Athene appears to Ulysses, lifts the fog just long enough to show him a view of Ithaca, helps him to hide the treasure in the cave, and warns him of the dangers awaiting him. She suggests his strategy. Ulysses should not reveal yet his identity, so she changes him into a pitiful-looking beggar clothed in rags. "Go unto the swineherd, who tends thy swine, and is loyal to thee as of old ... till I have gone to Sparta, the land of fair women, to call Telemachus thy dear son ... "

BOOK 14

Ulysses walks over a rough mountain path and finds the swineherd's house at "a place with wide prospect; a great court it was and a fair, with free range round it." Commentators seem to agree that the area is located at the southern tip of Ithaca. The swineherd does not recognize Ulysses who accounts for his presence on the island by pretending to be a Cretan and telling him a fake story. He says that he joined an expedition to the shore of the Nile River. They lost a battle and he was made prisoner. Seven years later a Phoenician, a "cunning liar," takes him to Phoenicia aboard a ship headed for Libya along the Cretan coast, pushed by a fair north wind (Boreas). At a point where they had left Crete behind and lost sight of all land, the ship is struck by lightning. Ulysses is the only one left alive, and drifts for nine days and nights clinging to the wreck. On the tenth day he reaches the land of the Thesprotians. The king of the Thesprotians advises him not to waste any time but to board a ship that is leaving for Dulichium, one of the islands near Ithaca. No sooner does the ship reach the open sea that the sailors strip Ulysses of his clothes and "prepare for him the day of slavery." As the ship docks at Ithaca in the evening, the prisoner manages to escape.

Eumaeus the swineherd listens to his visitor's story with great sympathy, feeds him, and tells him his own sad account of the long absence of his master, Ulysses, and the shameful behavior of the pretenders (suitors) who live off his master's lands. Ulysses tells the swineherd that the master of the house will soon be home. To convince Eumeus he is even offering him a bet. It is time for supper; the night falls, and Ulysses spends the night at the house of the swineherd.

BOOK 15

Athene, who has met Ulysses on the shore, goes to Sparta in the meantime to persuade Telemachus to return to Ithaca. She reveals to him in his dream the route he should follow in order to avoid the ambush the pretenders set for him between Ithaca and Cephalonia. Upon leaving sandy Pylos, Telemachus is instructed to steer north and keep away from the islands before setting a west course to Ithaca. Athene suggests that he should stay overnight at the house of Eumaeus the swineherd after dispatching his ship toward the city. The swineherd himself should be sent to the house of Ulysses to announce to Penelope the homecoming of her *son*. As Telemachus and the son of King Nestor get up at dawn, they say good-bye to Menelaus and Helen who offer them the usual gifts of hospitality and treat them to a meal before they get on the road in the chariot. "All

176 THE SECRET CODE OF THE ODYSSEY

day long they (the horses) swayed the yoke they bore upon their
necks. And the sun sank, and all the ways were darkened. And they
came to Pharae, to the house of Diocles. There they rested for the
night."

We learn from this episode that driving through the day Telemachus covers the same distance on the homeward trip as he did on his
way up, and that he again stays overnight at [Pharae.] This detail has
an important bearing on our interpretation of the story.

Soon as early Dawn shone forth, the rosy-fingered, they yoked
the horses and mounted the inlaid car. And forth they drave from
the gateway and the echoing gallery. Soon thereafter they reached
the steep hold of Pylos.

Telemachus asks the permission of the son of Nestor not to go up
to the Acropolis with him. "Leave me there, lest the old man keep
me in his house in my despite, out of his eager kindness, for I must
go right quickly home."

He is then heading straight for his ship realizing that Nestor will
be "very wroth . . . despite thine excuse." "Let us climb aboard," he
says, "that we may make way upon our course." They hoist the sail
while Athene sends them a fair wind. They pass in front of the
Fountains and the beautiful water of Chalcis. Meanwhile the sun had
set and all the ways were darkened; the ship, headed toward
[Pharae] was running swiftly thanks to the fair wind sent by Zeus.
They also pass Elis where the Epeans rule.

While this is happening, Ulysses and Eumaeus the swineherd
spend much of the night talking at the side of a wood fire inside the
hut. The swineherd tells him the story of his life. He was still a child
when the Phoenicians, "famous sailors, but greedy men" who came
to trade in his country, kidnapped him after swaying his nurse and
drawing her to their side as an accomplice. That is how, at some later
time, the Phoenicians sold him to Laertes, the father of Ulysses.
When the storytelling is over, Ulysses and Eumaeus go to sleep but
their sleep is brief. Dawn is beginning to break while at the shore
Telemachus and his men pull in the sails, moor the ship, and have
their first meal on Ithacan soil since leaving the island. Telemachus

orders them to "drive the black ship to the city, while I will go to
the fields and to the herdmen." The ship eventually pulls away from
the shore and heads toward the city of Ithaca by rounding the
southern tip of the island. Telemachus himself hurries up along the
path and soon reaches the place of Eumaeus the swineherd.

BOOK 16

The swineherd greets him at the threshold of his cabin, overwhelmed
with joy at seeing him. Telemachus comes in and sits down next to
Ulysses whom he doesn't recognize. He apologizes that he cannot
himself receive the stranger in his house, which is held by the
pretenders, and asks Eumaeus to put up the visitor at the farm for
the time being. It is now Ulysses' turn to express surprise that his
host Telemachus tolerates these goings-on in his own house. Telemachus explains how this situation has developed and asks the swineherd to go to Ulysses' house and tell Penelope that her son is safely
back from Pylos. "As for me, I will tarry here, and do thou return
hither when thou hast told the tidings to her alone; but of the other
Achaeans let no man learn it, for there be many that devise mischief
against me." Eumaeus suggests going by the long way in order to
notify also Laertes, Ulysses' father. Telemachus is absolutely opposed
to the idea: "When thou hast told the tidings, come straight back,
and go not wandering through the fields after Laertes. But speak to
my mother that with all speed she send forth the housedame her
handmaid, secretly, for she might bear tidings to the old man." The
swineherd takes off for the city.

At this moment Athene appears to Ulysses and advises him to
talk with his son and devise with him a way of getting rid of the
pretenders. She is very anxious to fight on their side. That is when
Ulysses finally reveals his identity to his son: "Thy father am I, for
whose sake thou sufferest many pains and groanest sore, and submit-
test thee to the despite of men." Telemachus is still not ready to
recognize him, for Athene has changed his father from a pitiful
beggar into a handsome man, an event that Ulysses takes care to
explain to his son. They eventually embrace one another. Ulysses

then wishes to know about the strength of his opponents. His son gives him an exact count of the pretenders of whom there are one hundred and eight, not counting their servants. Ulysses is certain of the assistance of Zeus and Athene and manages to reassure his son who would have preferred to round up some allies. Ulysses works out the details of his strategy, outlines them to his son, and gives him precise instructions, forbidding him to reveal to any one at all his presence on the island. Ulysses will take on again the form of a beggar when he knocks at the door of his own house.

While Ulysses and his son discuss the plans, Telemachus's ship enters the harbor of Ithaca. Once the ship is moored a messenger is dispatched to the house of Ulysses to advise Penelope according to the instructions of Telemachus. This messenger and Eumaeus the swineherd arrive at the same time at Penelope's room where they both convey to her their message. Once this is done the swineherd leaves immediately to join his herds. The pretenders are greatly surprised at the news that Telemachus is already back. They get together in front of the house and one of them suggests to notify their friends still laying in ambush on the sea that there is no point in waiting any longer. At this moment, as they look toward the port, they see the ship of their friends entering the harbor by rowing. They conclude that the men must have spotted Telemachus's ship from a distance but could not catch up with him. The pretenders assemble again in Ulysses' house and for the time being forget their plans to kill Telemachus. Penelope, who has learned that the pretenders were plotting the death of her son, comes down to face them and bitterly accuses them of their crime.

Ulysses and his son are questioning the swineherd as he gets back in the evening: "What news is there in the town? Are the lordly wooers now come home from their ambush or do they still watch for me yonder, to take me one my way home?" Eumaeus answers:

I had no mind to go about the city asking and inquiring hereof; my heart bade me get me home again, as quick as might be, when once I had told the tidings. And the swift messenger from thy company joined himself unto me, the henchman, who was the first to tell the news to thy mother. Yet this, too, I know, if thou wouldest hear; for I beheld it with mine eyes. Already had I come in my faring above the city, where is the hill Hermaean, when I marked a swift ship entering our haven, and many men there were in her, and she was laden with shields and two-headed spears, and methought they were the wooers.

The three men have dinner then and enjoy a good night's rest.

BOOK 17

Telemachus is the first to be on his way in the morning. At the house, he reassures his mother and tells her about his trip. Ulysses leaves a little later with the swineherd and knocks at the door of his house disguised as a beggar. Telemachus is kind to him and has food brought for the stranger who then turns toward the pretenders and asks them for alms. One of them abuses the swineherd for dragging a beggar into the house where they are having a good time. Despite a severe rebuke from Telemachus who takes Ulysses' part, the pretender strikes the beggar by throwing a footstool at him. Penelope learns about the beggar and wants to talk with him. Ulysses advises her to wait until nightfall so as not to rile the pretenders even more against him.

BOOK 18

Another beggar by the name of Iros is looking for a fight with Ulysses who is trying to calm him down: "I do not grudge that any should give to thee, yea though it were a good handful." But the beggar is in a angry mood and wants to chase Ulysses from the hall. The pretenders, of course, find this fighting funny and entertaining. Ulysses then accepts the challenge but makes the pretenders promise that they would not come to the beggar's rescue. The pretenders give their word at once; Ulysses knocks out Iros with a single punch and drags him outside. At this moment Athene inspires Penelope to appear once more before the pretenders. She warns her son not to associate with them any more and rebukes him for letting them mistreat a stranger. In the same breath she also criticizes the pretenders' attitude toward her, reminding them of the tradition that it is the pretender's duty to bring presents to a woman in order to influence her choice. Her speech and her beauty charm the pretenders so much that each of them orders his servant to bring a gift that they offer to the object of their desires. At nightfall the dinner ends with some more drinking and the pretenders finally leave the house. Ulysses remains inside under the pretext of tending to the candles.

BOOK 19

Father and son decide to take the arms off the walls where they are hanging to make sure that the pretenders will not be able to use these weapons against them. Telemachus will explain to them that he wanted to have the weapons cleaned. After this chore is done, Telemachus goes to bed while his mother comes down again to talk with Ulysses whom she hasn't recognized yet. She explains to him how much she is pining for Ulysses and how she has used every deceit to delay the moment when she would have to make a decision. She asks Ulysses where he comes from. Ulysses repeats to her the fantastic story that he is from Crete,

> a beautiful, luscious country surrounded by the sea; there are so many people living on the island that no one could count them; there are ninety cities, and people speak all the languages of the world. There are Achaeans there, along with proud Eteocretans, three tribes of Doriens, and noble Pelasgians. One of the cities is called Cnossos, and that is where Minos has been ruling since the age of nine.

The story is evidently a fictitious one, and it differs from the one he told Eumaeus. He claims to have met Ulysses at Crete before the hero left for Troy. To prove the authenticity of his witness, he gives a detailed account of the clothing Ulysses wore at the time: his robe, his brooch, his tunic. Penelope finally breaks down in tears and can longer doubt the stranger's word. Ulysses then tells her that her husband will soon be home: "He is safe and will come shortly." Penelope shows her gratitude by ordering her servants to look after the beggar's needs. An old nanny who used to know Ulysses well is summoned to bathe his feet. As she performs this duty, she recognizes a scar on Ulysses' leg dating back to the time when a wild boar he was hunting turned on him. Ulysses orders her not to tell anybody who he really is.

BOOK 20

As he lies down in the fore-hall and waits for sleep to come, he tries to figure out the best way to kill the pretenders. Athene puts his mind at ease, and he eventually goes to sleep. The next day a number of signs and omens forecast the imminent death of the pretenders. They are back again in the great hall. Telemachus warns them not to mistreat the beggar and takes this opportunity to remind them that they are in Ulysses' house. The assurance of Telemachus surprises and angers them. One of them goes so far as to suggest that they should put the beggar aboard a ship and send him to Sicily where he could be sold for good money.

BOOK 21

Penelope then suggests a contest with herself as a prize since they are so anxious to marry her. She has a servant bring out Ulysses' bow, which he left home when he went to Troy. She will marry the man who can string the bow the most skillfully and send an arrow through the holes of twelve axes lined up in a row. These ancient axes, in fact, were wrought in a way to leave a hole at the center of the blade. Telemachus lines up the axes, tries his hand at the bow, but soon gives up, admitting that he is not strong enough to string the bow properly. Each of the pretenders gives it a try without success. While this is going on inside, Ulysses is in the courtyard where he makes his identity known to Eumaeus and a cowherd who has remained faithful to him. Both of them promise to help him in the forthcoming battle. The pretenders are soon discouraged at their fruitless attempts and are ready to postpone the contest until the following day. At this point Ulysses asks for a chance to try the bow himself. The pretenders find this proposal outrageous, for they are afraid to be put to shame by a stranger who just might be able to bend Ulysses' bow. Penelope calms them down by promising that

even if the stranger won the contest, that did not mean that he
would also win the prize. Telemachus asks his mother to leave the
hall. He hands the bow to Ulysses while the faithful servants carefully
lock the doors and send the maids outside. Ulysses strings the bow
and sends the arrow through the row of the dozen axes. Telemachus,
armed with a spear, is at his side; the two of them stand at the hall
door with the loaded quiver at their feet.

BOOK 22

Ulysses shoots Antinous, the leader of the pretenders, in the throat.
Stupor and panic seize all those present. The others still believe that
the shooting was an accident, and they threaten Ulysses who picks
this moment to reveal his true identity. The pretenders are stricken
with terror and try to save their lives by accusing the dead Antinous
and promising reparation. "Not even so would I henceforth hold my
hands from slaying," says Ulysses mercilessly. Fighting remains their
only choice. The pretenders try to get close to Ulysses but are struck
down one after the other.

Ulysses is running out of arrows and he suspects that the pretenders who are still alive may have received some weapons through one
of their servants. The situation is critical. Telemachus and the two
faithful servants go to look for weapons in the storeroom. Athene
lends her help and deflects the spears as the pretenders throw them.

The fight is definitely turning now in Ulysses' favor. Only two
men, a harper and a messenger who used to look after Telemachus
when he was a child, give Ulysses a chance to exercise clemency on
the intervention of Telemachus.

The massacre of the pretenders ends. Their blood flows all over
the hall, and the spectacle is awful to behold. Ulysses summons the
old nanny who had recognized him and asks her which of the women
of the house had compromised themselves with the pretenders.
"Twelve out of fifty," says the old maid. Ulysses then charges her to
order all of these women into the hall. He forces them to drag the
bodies into the courtyard and clean the hall. After that the women
are hanged in a corner of the yard. The goatherd who betrayed

Ulysses and brought the weapons to the pretenders suffers a longer and more horrible death.

BOOK 23

Penelope can hardly believe the old nurse who tells her what has just happened. She is afraid to believe that Ulysses has really come back and thinks that only an immortal god could have prevailed over the pretenders. The nanny then tells her how she had recognized Ulysses by the scar on his leg. Penelope then comes down to the hall, still not sure about Ulysses. Telemachus accuses her of being cold while Ulysses leaves the hall to get bathed and make himself more presentable. He comes back, but Penelope is still on her guard, full of distrust. Ulysses finally finds the one sure way of allaying all her doubts. He reminds her of the time when he built their chamber around an olive tree that he then cut down with his own hands, fashioning the lumber into their conjugal bed. Doubt is no longer possible, and Penelope throws herself into his arms.

A while later Ulysses cannot help revealing to her that their trials have not ended yet. Tiresias the soothsayer, whom he conjured up at the land of the Cimmerians, had predicted that he would have his home again to live out his life far from his country and from the sea. He spends the night with Penelope, but he is in a hurry to leave the house and look for his old father Laertes before the news of the massacre of the pretenders spreads over the island.

BOOK 24

The *Odyssey* could well end right here, and some of the commentators have offered several arguments to show that this last Book is not genuine. The souls of the pretenders descend into Hades to meet Achilles and Agamemnon and tell under what circumstances they died as a result of Ulysses' homecoming.

Meanwhile Ulysses and Telemachus find Laertes who tells the man he takes for a stranger how he resented the intrusion of the pretenders and how sad he was over his lost son. Once more Ulysses wishes to try the other person before revealing himself. After giving vent to the usual emotions, Laertes is suddenly seized by fear: "My heart is terribly afraid, lest straightway all the men of Ithaca come up against us here, and haste to send messengers everywhere to the cities of the Cephalonians." These lines clearly imply that the cause of Ulysses is not very popular on Ithaca and on the islands. News of the pretenders' death, in fact, spread rapidly. The Ithacans bury their dead and then hurry to the *agora*(marketplace)for a general assembly. Eupeithes, father of Antinous the pretender, who was the first one slayed by Ulysses, speaks up:

> Friends, a great deed truly hath this man devised against the Achaeans. Some with his ships he led away, many men and noble, and his hollow ships hath he lost, and utterly lost of his company, and others again, and those far the best of the Cephalonians he hath slain on his coming home. . . . Up, let us be going, lest these fellows be beforehand with us and over the sea.

Fortunately, the two men whose life Ulysses has spared appear before the assembly and speak against such punitive measures, reminding the audience that the gods were manifestly on Ulysses' side in his undertaking. Half of the people give up their plans and go home discouraged. The other half grab their weapons and follow Eupeithes into a new battle. Ulysses kills Eupeithes with his spear. At this moment Athene intervenes and stops the fighting with her powerful voice that frightens the warring party. That is how peace returns on the island of Ithaca.

REFERENCE NOTES

HOMER
Les Premières Civilisations de la Méditerranée
par Gabriel Leroux. (P.U.F.)
Chapter II, p. 5
The choice is as hard as ever between the theory of a staff of minstrels such as the Homerides of Chios, or a single poetic genius . . . Homer is generally placed at 850 B.C. The Homeric language seems to be essentially Aeolian, modified at a later time by the Ionian dialect. The *Iliad* and the *Odyssey* acquired a more or less definite form after the Athens census carried out by the order of Pisistratus in 560.

SPATIAL DIRECTIONS AND ZODIACAL SIGNS
Géographie sacrée de monde grec
by Jean Richer (Bibl. des Guides Bleus)
p.55
The fig leaf symbolizes the mystical tree and indicates the south-north axis.
p. 73
Artemis the huntress is a reference to Sagittarius.

PROHISTORICAL DATA
Manuel de Préhistoire Générale(Bibliothèque scientifique)
by Raymond Furon (Payot, Paris)
Sea Levels
p. 51
Chronological calculations yield the conclusion that in the North Sea marine transgression reaches the figure minus 35 before

the year 15000 in the Magdalanian. Around minus 7000 or minus 8000 the sea is at minus 20, submerging Pas de Calais. A little later at Yoldia the sea invades the Baltic Lake, which once again becomes Lake Ancylus.

Toward minus 6500 the transgression reaches minus 10. Toward minus 4000 the sea level is at the present zero.

Toward the third and fourth centuries the coasts of Brittany are submerged. At that time the city of Ys in the bay of Douarnenez is submerged.

After a standstill lasting several centuries and followed by a slight recession, the sea rises again to submerge the Netherlands in the twelfth and thirteenth centuries.

At Plogoff Point (Brittany), megalithic monuments are being discovered under six meters of water.

The climatical optimum of the Neolithic Age started in minus 5400.

Cretans

Trade is very active from Ancient Minoan I (2800 to 24000). Crete is organized and is on its way toward becoming a great power. Industrial utilization of bronze contributes to the importance and power of Crete, which undertakes exportation of tin from the west. Cretan sailors venture to Sicily and into the Adriatic. Greece is 200 years behind Crete in the bronze industry.

Troy

The bronze of common usage contains 10 per cent tin. Lapis lazuli from Afghanistan and amber from the Baltic area were also found.

Treasure finds include a large variety of jewelry, some with exotic designs proving the existence of extended trade with all of the east, the Mediterranean, the Danube basin, and the Baltic area.

Mycenaeans

The Mycenaeans conquer, sack, and burn Cnossos toward 1400. Mycenae thus becomes the successor of Crete.

Trade relations are established toward the west with Italy, Sicily, Sardinia, and Spain.

Aegean sailors, whose stopovers were discovered in Sicily and southern Italy, introduced bronze to the Iberian Peninsula at the beginning of the second millenium.

Great Britain

p. 402

At the dawn of this same second millenium a group of Celts descend along the Rhine and settle in Great Britain.

The Goideles, or Gaels, who brought bronze to Great Britain for the first time were later pushed back to Ireland and Scotland.

Sicily

p. 410

Sicilian civilization of the second millenium is divided into Sicilian I (from minus 2000 to minus 15000) and Sicilian II (from minus 1500 to the end of the millenium). During Siclian II the province is drawn into the Mycenaean trade system and Sicilian economy changes into Bronze Age economy. From that age Aegean vases from Helladic III, mirrors, bronze swords, and golden rings are found in Sicily. Local craftsmen imitate sword styles of Late Mycenaean I (Crete), hollow axes and Trojan knives, and later double-edged razors and buckles.

Sun Cult

p. 411

The most important find testifying to sun cult in the Aegaean area is a silver engraving discovered in Syron, displaying a solar chariot. The sun cult spread as far as Scaninavia.

Cult of the Double Ax or [Bipennis]

p. 413

This symbol of lightning and thunder (Zeus) is found in the palace of Cnossos in Greece. It is also found in Northern Italy, in the Balearics, Spain, Brittany, and Scandinavia.

MATHEMATICAL KNOWLEDGE

De la préhistoire à l'histoire (What Happened in History)

by Gordon Childe

1. p. 176

In the valley of the Nile, scribes during the second millenium (B.C.) copied medical prescriptions and arithmetical problems that they identify as originating from the third millenium . . . A certain Ahmes in the fifteenth century proudly states that his book on arithmetics is based on a text dating back to the time of king Amenemhat (1880-1850 B.C.) . . . Formulas used by the administrators of the Sumer temples and by Egyptian architects enabled them, by application of the laws of mathematics and mechanics, to figure the quantities of grain needed to seed their fields and the number of stones needed for constructing their pyramids. The Egyptian calendar and its correction by Sirius show true application of the laws of quantitative astronomy.

2. p. 233

Toward 1800 B.C., the Babylonians discovered, through direct observation and measuring, certain geometric relations besides the ones used in calculating surface and volume, which they had known for a long time . . . Scribes knew of nineteen different applications of the Pythagorean theorem.

TROY

Premières Civilisations de la Méditerranée
by Gabriel Leroux (P.U.F.)

Chapter II, p. 5

Troy, with its art and civilization that closely paralleled that of the Mycenaeans, was their fearsome rival on the Asia Minor markets. The siege is generally dated between 1193 and 1184 B.C.

. . . In all probability, the objective of the Achaean expedition was to destroy the main power that stood in the way of their expansion in Asia Minor. From the twelfth century on, in fact, entire cities and tribes embark for Asia Minor, taking along their gods, their riches, their traditions, including many secrets of the Cretan civilization that they preserved through the Mycenaean period.

The First colonists were Achaeans (Aeolians) who left Epiros and Etolia in the west and Thessalia and Boetia in the East, to cross the Aegean Sea and settle between the straits and gulf of Smyrna around 1150.

THE ATLANTIC ROUTE

Ulysses est-il allé en Bretagne?

by Robet Philippe (The review *Planète, no. 22.*)

"Our Theory: The Odyssey in the Atlantic"

Since the *Iliad* presents no mysteries, the debate is confined to the *Odyssey*. The Iliad is the story of a victorious military operation against the guardians of the straits through which the Greeks are seeking a free route toward the Black Sea . . . Ulysses is the symbol of this Greek adventure . . . The adventure story reveals a certain lack of continuity. After an easy return trip until Cape Malea, a storm creates a nine-day blank at the end of which Ulysses, after losing his bearings, suddenly appears with his ships in the middle of an archipelago.

Was this a Mediterranean archipelago? In all probability, no. Commentators have arbitrarily fixed the place of this second departure within the Mediterranean and thus warped all subsequent interpretations. The storm has pushed Ulysses outside the Mediterranean, into the Atlantic. Ulysses thus finds himself on the fabulous but very real sea route of gold, tin, and amber.

With Book 5 of the *Odyssey* begins the narrative of an Atlantic expedition . . . Where did the narrator find the geographical data he uses? In some Phoenician travel account or a kind of oral sea chart? In any event, the data concerning the coasts and the ocean are Phoenician in origin.

NAVIGATIONAL POSSIBILITIES

De la préhistoire à l'histoire

by Gordon Childe.

p. 226

1. During the second millenium . . . improved transportation facilities made communication by land and sea easier. As early as in the Middle Empire, Egyptians were able to build ships 61 meters long by 20 meters wide that could transport 120 persons. Cretan vessels that had been only 20 meters long grow to 30 meters in the Mycenaean period. During the fair season a sea trip from the delta ports of the Nile to Byblos took four days . . .

p. 283

2. The seafaring Greeks used the stars as guides and were able to observe certain celestial phenomena that their priests, living on land in their temples, missed. The sailors have noticed that on trips to the south the polar star seemed to drop closer and closer to the horizon. They could calculate the distance they covered by measuring the height of the star, that is, its angle with the horizon. The Greeks benefited by the astronomical discoveries of the Babylonians and Egyptians. There existed a long dictionary of the names of the stars in the library of the Hittite capital as early as in the second millenium B.C.

ANCIENT NAVIGATION
Histoire de la navigation
by Pierre Célérier (P.U.F.)

Chapter I, p. 11

Use of the polar star as navigational guide goes back to prehistory.

Chapter II

The Egyptian ship is the first type of these long vessels that dominated the Mediterranean for centuries. Its direct descendant is the Greek trireme.

The trireme sped to an attack at a maximum speed of some ten knots, propelled by eight-eight oars at which one hundred and forty-four oarsmen were straining their muscles . . .

Ancient rupestrine paintings discovered in Scandinavia show that inhabitants of that area ventured on the high seas as early as three to four thousand years before Christian times.

There are reasons to think that at some time in history the world was better known than in subsequent ages. That is, for instance, how the rich and legendary Tarchiech mentioned in the Bible really existed . . . very probably in Spain, at the mouth of the Guadalquivir where it was a seaport founded about thirty centuries before Christian times. Some even think that ships sailing out of this port, and later from Carthage, regularly visited Madeira and the Canaries, which were officially rediscovered by Portuguese seamen toward A.D. 1350

It has been firmly established that lands were known and regularly visited long before their official date of discovery, the primary example being America. There is no reason why the same phenomenon could not have happened at earlier ages. The secrecy surrounding these early discoveries would be a sufficient explanation.

ANCIENT NAVIGATION—TECHNICAL CONDITIONS
Histoire de la navigation
by Pierre Célérier (P.U.F.)
Chapter III, p. 1.

History has demonstrated that great sea voyages had taken place long before our own era. It has also demonstrated that people have visited almost regularly lands separated by thousands of kilometers of sea without any sophisticated means of high-sea navigation.

People have been watching the heavens and have followed the movements of the stars from the earliest ages. In any event, we know for certain that several peoples, such as the Egyptians, possessed an extensive and exact astronomical knowledge several thousand years before our time. Navigators used the azimuth of the sun and the stars at different seasons and at different hours of the day with sufficient approximation to find their way on the seas.

Our school-bred habit of not applying our curiosity beyond classical antiquity often prevents us from seeing the enormous stretches of preceding and perhaps equally civilized ages. Yet we have every reason to suppose that periods of civilization have been erased from man's memory; and, doubtless, navigation was practiced then as well as during historical times . . .
Chapter IV, p. 1

Real sea ports appear very soon in man's history. The first one we know in detail is Pharos in front of Alexandria, which the Egyptians built some three thousand years before Christ. The dikes totaled 8 kilometers, the basins covered 120 hectares of water and could accommodate eight hundred galleys . . . These dimensions are comparable to our own modern ports.

MARITIME GUIDES
Histoire de la navigation
by Pierre Célérier
Chapter III, p. 1

The Greeks confined all seafaring between March and October.

Knowledge of the results of former experiences was useful. That is how those collections were born that eventually became our guides on navigation. Such collections must have existed at all ages. They must have been transmitted orally from generation to generation, even before man learned how to write them down. People recited them in some versified form, which would account for the fact that the most ancient among these guides use a symbolic, poetic language. Although examples have reached us from all ages, most of them have certainly been lost since those who knew them considered them as secret information not to be divulged.

Scandinavian sagas that have reached us often refer to information they do not actually reveal. When they do give details, they seem to be speaking of routine trips . . .

Likewise, it is certain today that fishermen from the French coast frequented Newfoundland's coast several centuries before the official discovery of America. Yet one finds no trace of information about that navigation; the sailors must have jealously kept the secrets for themselves. The psychology of seafaring people did not change much through the ages.

ACHAEANS AND CRETANS
–MARITIME ROUTES OF THE ACHAEANS
Les premières civilisations de la Méditerranée
by Gabriel Leroux (P.U.F.)
Chapter II, 4./p. 59

When the Achaeans arrived in Greece around 2000, they did not know anything about the sea. Soon, however, we find them sailing along the same routes as the sailors of Crete and pushing forth along new routes toward the west.

As this happens, the Lucky Island (Crete) is in danger; the destruction of Cnossos around 1400 spells the death of Minoan Crete . . . The victors, however, become the actual heirs of Minoan civilization and extend its influence for two more centuries.

During this period, the Argolides, with their more advanced civilization, hold all of Greece under a more or less absolute rule. The fortified castles of the Pelopides at Mycenae, and the sons of Danaos at Tirynthe and Argos are rivals for power and splendor . . . The wealthy masters, owners of tremendous gold stocks, employ artisans who "continue to produce golden and silver jewelry noted for fine craftsmanship, and weaponry remains worthy of the daggars of Damascus and Cretan swords." However, Mycenaean art on the whole becomes vulgarized and industrialized. Workshops spring up all over the cities and around the palaces. Networds of busy roads cover Greece; maritime connections develop. Large-scale production with simplified manufacturing methods serves a market that is larger but whose artistic demands are more modest . . .

Even if we cannot say for certain that Cretans frequented the western Mediterranean markets, numerous traces of an Aegean influence there prove that the Mycenaeans did not fear those faraway expeditions. The first stop westward was, no doubt, corcyre (Corfu). Malta's and Sicily's debt to Aegean influences has already been noted . . . The Mycenaeans next went to the Aeolian islands to buy [liparite,] then to Sardinia where they sold copper ingots that bore Aegean seals, then to the Balearics, etc. On the Iberian coasts, the designs, jewels, and other objects of Egyptian style, which the Mycenaeans imitated for exportation, bring us perhaps to the kingdom of Tartessos . . .

It has not been established with certainty that the Mycenaeans knew Spain and the Pillars of Hercules. But even if they did, Greek seamen definitely did not know these faraway routes until the day when a storm pushes Kolaios of Samia into Tartessos in 630. He comes back with a fabulous shipload of gold on which he makes a profit of 60 talents.

MYCENAEAN TRADE
De la préhistoire à l'histoire
by Gordon Childe.

In Mycenaean Greece . . . merchants made substantial profits, and had access to high social standing . . .

After 1400 B.C., Mycenaean commerce succeded the Minoan . . . Mycenaeans exported pottery toward Troy, the southwest coast of Asia Mnior, Syria, Egypt, Palestine, Sicily, and Italy.

Mycenaean commerce then turned toward uncivilized Europe. The pottery reached Macedonia and Sicily and went farther still. Faience beads fashionable in 1400 were found as far as southern England. A Greek-made dagger has been discovered in a Bronze Age mound in Cornwall, In exchange, Mycenaeans imported tin from Cornwall, gold from Ireland, and ornaments made in England . . .

Thus from that time the uncivilized lands, including Ireland and Denmark, made a positive contribution to the collective human experience whose home was the Near East.

It is possible that the Bronze Age civilizations of Western and Central Europe were born of this proved commercial activity; in any case, the contacts favored their development. As an example, the barbarian aristocrats of southern England and Denmark, grown rich by the commerce with faraway lands, were the sociological and economic equivalents of the Mycenaean leaders. Assuredly, they were poorer and more provincial; but the contacts between the Nordic aristocracy and the wealthy Minoan world probably contributed to the birth of Greece's heroic age.

SICILY AND SARDINIA
La civilisation de la Méditerranée
by J. Gabriel Leroux (P.U.F.)

In Sicily
1. p. 24

Ceramics with brown, black, or white designs on red background, curious spiral motifs on large stones that serve to close the entrance to tombs, and an engraved golden plaque, replica of one found at the second city of Hissarlik (Troy) bear witness to connections with the Aegean area and indicate that this period ought to be placed between about 2500 and 1900.

Commerce seems to stop for several centuries after which a second Sicilian period opens (1400 to 1000) coinciding with the Mycenaean expansion. The following archeological finds at ·the Syracuse area point to steady commerce: Mycenaean vases, glass beads, probably of Egyptian origin, and porphcy pyxis bearing the name of Ramses II, 1300-1235.

Sardinia

2. p. 30

The most flourishing period coincides with the Bronze Age at the time of the Mycenaean expansion, which, no doubt, has contributed to the development of metallurgy in Sardinia. Ingots of Cyprian copper have been found there as well as bronze axes and swords worthy of their prototypes from Cnossos (Crete) and Mycenae (Greece).

MARITIME CONNECTIONS (TARTESSOS)
Les Civilisations de la Méditerranée
by J. Gabriel Leroux (P.U.F.)

Spain

p. 28

Contact with the Atlantic countries, especially Ireland, is more certain. That explains the rapid growth of bronze metallurgy, probably introduced from the east, as copper was from 2000 on. From that time the Spaniards must have sought not only Galician tin but also the tin of Cornwall, the famous Cassiteride islands of the Ancients . . .

The Tartessians occupy (Beatic) and Andalusia, the richest regions of Spain. As famous metalworkers and bold sailors who knew well the Atlantic coast, they received at Tartessos, their capital city built at the mouth of the Guadalquivir, merchants attracted from all points of the Mediterranean by their reputation for their fabulous wealth and by their commerce in silver and tin.

Their generous hospitality, their energetic and refined civilization, comparable in its imposing luxury to that of the Orient, deeply impressed the ancients. According to Strabon, their civilization goes back 6000 years. He praises their poems and the rhymed annals preserved by their priests.

CANARY ISLANDS
Les Pays Légendaires
by René Thévenin (P.U.F.)
Chapter II, p. 4

Jean de [Béthencourt] takes possession of the Canary Islands where a Genovese expedition landed in 1341. They made a very unusual discovery there. A strange people lived on the island. Although they were of white race, their body type and their language bore no resemblance to anything known. They wore no clothes, lived in caves, did not know any metals, and the only tools or weapons they used were of wood or stone. They had no notion of seafaring.

Chapter 3, p. 4

The Guanches were tall men with white skin, blond hair, and light eyes. Their body type has nothing in common with the African races living at the same latitudes. An examination of their skeletons reveals that their oblong cranium, high forehead, and low and triangular face place them in the family of our own Cro-Magnon ancestors.

THE GUANCHES
Les Isles Canaries
by Arielle et Castro Farinas (Albin Michel)
p. 35

Since the most distant times, the Canaries were inhabited by a very industrious white race, the Guanches ... Guanche mummies show that the people were tall, 1.80 meters at least, with blond or brown hair. It is thought that they had blue eyes ...

They lived in natural caves or in huts with roofs made of plants ... A study of the skeletons found at burial sites confirms that the inhabitants were unusually strong, with an almost super-human vitality and resistance.

... in conclusion, after a first wave of Cro-Magnon men of Euro-African type whose culture is very ancient, other peoples settled the island; they were Mediterraneans of an easterly type, armenoid, slender; others yet followed, importing a more advanced culture.

... the Guanches of Tenerife and of Gomera embalmed their dead in the same way as the Egyptians and the Peruvians of pre-Columbian times.

p. 39

In 1341 a Portuguese expedition sails toward the islands. Only five of the thirteen islands they explore are inhabited.

p. 88

The Seven Canary Islands

Chapter 64, *The Canaries*, by [Jean de Béthencourt,] History of the Discovery in 1402.

The Canary Islands are seven ... the first, when one comes from Castile, is Lanzarote, rich in wheat and animals, especially goats. It would be a good land for grapes and trees, but they do not grow because the many grazing cattle destroy everything.. There is no fresh water.

Farther, Fuerteventura: it is rich in fresh river water. There are many goats, few cows, some grapes, vegetable gardens, almond and other trees; it is located three leagues from Lanzarote.

The great Canary is immediately after: a large island, rich in fresh river water, with much sugar cane, corn, wheat, barley, wine, fig trees, and many date trees.

Tenerife is next ... where there is a chain of the highest mountains of the world; upon the peaks, flames appear sometimes as at Mongibel in Sicily.

TRADE RELATIONS BETWEEN ENGLAND AND
THE MEDITERRANEAN AT THE BRONZE AGE
L'Age du Bronze
by Jacques Briard (P.U.F.)

p. 59

The most advanced civilization in England at the end of the ancient Bronze Age is the civilization of Wessex.

Its most important feature is its commerce with the faraway regions of Central Europe, the Aegean area, and even Egypt . . .

p. 61

Glass or faience beads embedded in peat are among the interesting archeological finds. They were imported from the Egyptian workshops of Tell el Arna. Their geographical distribution prompted H. C. Beck and J. F. Stone to date the Wessex findings at around minus 1400.

One of the engravings at Stonehenge shows a Mycenaean-type dagger, which confirms the connections between the England of the Early Bronze with the Mediterranean civilizations.

OXEN HIDES–INGOTS
L'Age du Bronze
by Jacques Briard (P.U.F.)

p. 122

The raw material travels under many different forms.

In the Mediterranean, the ruling Cretans monopolized the copper trade. The stocks of metal were kept in ingots shaped like oxen hides and often bore favorite Cretan emblems such as the double ax.

p. 117

In Sardinia, the islands' own ores were used; however, Aegean ingots in the shapes of oxen hides show that Aegean prospectors were the ones to introduce the metallurgical techniques there.

IRISH GOLD AND TRADE CONNECTIONS OF IRELAND
L'Age due Bronze
by Jacques Briard (P.U.F.)

1. p. 38

Civilizations of the Ancient Bronze were somewhat prosperous; gold at times was used extensively and even served as the basis of significant trading such as the Irish lunule.

2. p. 59

In the early Bronze Age, Ireland knew a very active metallurgical industry. Gold is one of the most sought-after Irish products in the Early Bronze Age. It is exported to England and to continental Europe in crescent-shaped flat sheets called lunules, gorgets, or diadems . . . Toward the end of the Early Bronze Age, another original Irish product is the ax, flat or appearing with raised edges, decorated on the flat surfaces as well as along the raised edges with geometric designs, chevrons, diamond shapes, etc. Axes of this type have been found from western France to Northern Europe. Irish gold continues to be traded through the Middle Bronze Age.

SOURCES OF PREHISTORIC TIN SUPPLIES
Le Problème des Cassitérides
by Jacques Ramin (Editions Picard).

p. 25

The abundance of tin in the British Isles is well known. Much of this wealth is concentrated in Cornwall and in the southeast of Devonshire. That is, in fact, the area that is thought to have generated the most important tin production before Christian times . . .

p. 26

Some tin is found also in Ireland, at Wisklow where it appears together with gold, a product the ancient Irish exported at protohistorical times. Also at Ballina . . .

p. 28

Bronze appears in Crete toward 2400 B.C. Its use soon becomes very popular. At that time the Cretans have already a merchant marine and carry on commercial operations in the whole Mediterranean basin, perhaps as far as Spain . . .

This very expansion toward the west, well established at the time of the development of Cretan bronze production, creates a presumption that the tin supplies were obtained from a western source . . .

p.42

We point out incidentally that a metallurgical industry existed in Ireland; toward the end of the Early Bronze, flat axes and axes with raised and decorated edges were being exported to western France and Northern Europe. The civilization of southern Wessex shows trade with Central Europe, the Aegean area, and Egypt.

WHAT PREHISTORIC TIN LOOKED LIKE
Le Problème des Cassitérides
by Jacques Ramin (Editions Picard)

Tin-bearing minerals appear as impregnations, small veins, or alluvial grains. To this day the most important tin finds appear in these forms ... which is the case of marine alluvions: The action of the waves produces a thorough mixture of the various alluvions ... The sea washes the mineral, which is then deposited on the beach in a concentrated enough form to be visible to the naked eye, and allows processing without mechanical means ...

While speaking of tin and of protohistorical times, let us not forget that Europe was covered with forests, but immense stretches of the coastline were well known. This makes us think that alluvions, especially marine alluvions, were the first and most easily detected sources of supply.

Agitation by the sea sorts out the minerals by gravity. The material thus rearranged appears in the form of long lines of a deeper color, easily observable on the white sand.

LOCATION OF THE CASSITERIDE ISLANDS
Le Problème des Cassitérides
by Jacqurs Ramin (Editions Picard)

p. 53

Some (historical documents) place the Cassiterides far away, to the north of Spain.

p. 56

All authors place the Cassiterides, or, when the name itself is not used, the sources of tin supply in Western Europe.

p. 58

Herodotus (Vth century B.C.)

I have no information on the Cassiterides.... I have not heard from any eyewitness that a sea existed beyond the confines of Europe. The only certain fact is that our electrum (amber) comes from far away countries of that part of the world.

Eustachius calls Ireland "Ibernia," that is, country of the Ibernians.

Avienus (orbis descriptio) speaks of the Iberians that reach up to the cold waters of the North Ocean.

Pliny Senior says: Facing Celtiberia there are several islands that the Greeks call Cassiterides after the tin mines that exist there (IV, 36-1).

The first tin was imported from the Cassiterides by Nidacritus (VII, 57-7).

p. 59

We think with S. Remiach (*Un nouveau texte sur le commerce de l'étain*) that the Phoenicians were not the first ones to import tin. The title of first importer may have been given to the Phrygian Midas only because the surviving memory of a very ancient tradition going back before the tenth century when Midas is supposed to have lived.

p. 60

Strabon (II, 5, 15)

In his general description of the Ibernian Peninsula, Strabon mentions that the Western parts of England are situated on the far side, toward the north. He adds that the islands called Cassiterides are located to the north of the Artabres (Galicia), at about the same area.

Strabon (III, 5, 11)

There are ten Cassiteride islands, located in the high seas North of the port of Artabres (La Coruña), and are all very close to one another. One of them is desert ... They (the people of the islands) produce tin and lead that they exchange ...

Herodotus (Fifth century B.C.)

p. 61

who lived in the second century A.D., gives the coordinates of the Cassiteride islands, are supposed to be located in the ocean to the north-west of the Iberian Peninsula.

Avienus (Ora Maritima)

p. 67

was based on very old Carthaginian documents ...

From there (Oestrymmis) it takes two day to reach the Sacred Island (Ireland), as it used to be called, which takes up a large portion of the sea as the country of the Hibernian people. The island of the Albions is nearby. Trade expeditions from Tartessos (southern Spain) used to go all the way to the Oestrymmides.

Himilcon was commissioned by Carthage, as was Hannon toward 600 B.C., to scout the Atlantic coasts north of the Pillars of Hercules. He has definitely visited Brittany ... His voyage took four months, and he had the time to reach the British Isles.

Pytheas, a Greek from Marseilles, sailed around Great Britain toward 323 B.C., advancing to the island of Thula, which touches the Arctic Circle.

BIBLIOGRAPHY

1. TRANSLATIONS

M. Dufour et J. Raison. *L'Odyssée*. Garnier Flammarion. Paris 1965

Ph. Jaccottet. *L'Odyssée*. Club Français due Livre. Paris 1965

E. Lasserre. *L'Iliade*. Garnier Flammarion. Paris 1965

2. COMMENTARIES

Ph. Champault. *Le Calembour, l'énigme et l'allégorie dans Homère*. Mercure de France. Novembre 1913

Ch. Mugler. *Les Origines de la Science grecque chez l'Homme et l'Univers. Physique d'Homère*. Paris 1963

V. Bérard. *L'Odyssée d'Homère. Étude et analyse*
—— *Les Navigations d'Ulysse*. Armand Colin, Paris 1928
—— *Les Phéniciens et l'Odyssée*. Paris 1927

Th. H. Martin. *Les longs jours et les longues nuits des Lestrygons*
=== *Annuaire des Études grecques*. 1878

R. Herbenrath. *Die Polarfahrt des Odysseus.* Stuttgarter Zeitung. 1926

U. von Wilamowitz. Moellendorff. *Die Heimkehr des Odysseus*. Berlin 1927

K. Jarz. *Wo sind die Homerischen Inseln?* Wien 1882

R. Reinhard. *Die Erzählung des Odyssée*. Wien 1916

P. Tamery. *Sur la Géographie de l'Odyssée.* Faculté de Bordeaux 1887

K. Breusing. *Die Irrfahrten des Odysseus*

F. Walter. *Die Odyssee und die Odysseusage*

R. Philippe. *Ulysse est-il allé en Bretagne?* Planete (revue). Paris. Mai 1965

3. ANCIENT NAVIGATION

Lelewel. *Pythéas de Marseille*. Paris 1837

E. Courbaud. *La navigation d'Hercule*. Rome 1892

Moreau de Jonnès. *L'Océan des Anciens*. Paris 1873

J. Courcelle Seneuil. *Heraclès: Les Égéens sur les côtês occidentales de l'Europe vers le svie siècle*. Paris 1915

Oppert-Tharsisch und Ophir. Berlin

A. Anthiaume. *Les cartes marines dans l'antiquité*. Bulletin géogr. et hist. 1912

────── . *Évolution de la science nautique en France*. Paris 1920

M. Cary et E. Warnington. *Les explorateurs de l'antiquité*. Paris 1926

P.E. Hermann. *L'homme à la découverte du monde*. Payot 1952

R. de Loture. *La navigation à travers les âges*. Payot 1952

────── *Itinéraires maritimes occidentaux dans l'antiquité*

──────*Bulletin de l'Association des Géogr. anciens*. Paris 1954

J. Vars. *L'art nautique dans l'antiquité*

P. Celerier. *Histoire de la Navigation*. P. U. F. Paris 1956

R. Thevenin. *Les pays légendaires*. P. U. F. Paris 1961

4. PREHISTORY

H. Hirmenich. *Les Celtes, l'Atlantide et les Atlantes*. Paris 1906

G. Bonsor. *Tartessos*. Madrid 1921

Hildebrandt. *Sur la situation des Cassitérides*. Stockholm 1874

G. Glotz. *La civilisation Égéenne*, Paris 1923

L. Siret. *Les Cassitérides et l'empire colonial des Phéniciens*

────── *L'anthropologie*. 1908 a 1910

Ch. Picard. *Les origines du Polythéisme hellénique*. Paris 1930

J. Briard. *L'âge du Bronze* P. U. F. Paris

Rivaud. *Timée et Critias*. Paris 1925

G. Leroux. *Les premières civilisations de la Méditerranée*. P. U. F. 1961

Y. Lissner. *Ainsi vivaient nos ancêtres*. Corrêa. Paris 1957

G. Childe. *De la Préhistoire à l'histoire*. Gallimard. Paris 1963

J. Ramin. Le Problême des Cassiterides. E. Picard. Paris 1965

H. Harrel Courtes. *Les fils de Minos*. Plon. Paris 1967

R. Furon. *Manuel de la Préhistoire Générale*. Payot. Paris

J. Mazel. *Avec les Phéniciens* . . . R. Laffont. Paris

5. GEOGRAPHY

D.G. Hogarth. *Iona and the East*. Oxford 1909

J. Richer. *Géographie sacrée du Monde Grec*. Hachette. Paris 1966

Arielli et Castro Farinas. *Les Iles Canaries*. Albin Michel. Paris 1966

W.H. Murray. *The Hebrides Heinemann*. London 1966

H.H. Scullard. *Petit atlas de l'antiquité classique*. Édition Sequoia. Paris

INDEX OF PLACE NAMES

205